Not Necessarily in Them Thar Hills

*Moonshine Stories
from the Middle Peninsula and Northern Neck of Virginia*

by Robert F. Watkins

Not Necessarily in Them Thar Hills
Moonshine Stories from the Middle Peninsula and Northern Neck of Virginia
Robert F. Watkins

ISBN: 978-0-6159067-8-2 (Watkins)

Published by
Robert F. Watkins
P.O. Box 397
Tappahannock, Virginia 22560
(804) 443-3213

All Rights Reserved. This book or parts thereof may not be reproduced in any form, without written permission of the author except as provided by the United States of America copyright law.

Printed by
Barbour Printing Services, Inc.
Tappahannock, Virginia
December 2013

Third Printing

Cover photo by Dawn Howeth, *Picture This by Dawn*.

Acknowledgements

Thanks to *Professor Joseph Swonk* for his support;
Barbara Nannery for taking her time to help organize
and arrange the array of papers that have turned into this book;
James Blanks and *The House & Home Magazine* for
generating interest in the community and
jump-starting this process;
Robin Harmon, my daughter, who has put in many long hours
and stuck by me for many months;
Lindsay Harmon, my granddaughter, who without her, this book
would never have been written and for her determination to help
make this lifelong dream a reality;
and my wife, wonderful family and friends who have listened
to story after story and have encouraged me
to push on in spite of many obstacles.

Table of Contents

Preface ix

Introduction xi

Chapter I:
The History of Prohibition, Moonshining, and Virginia ABC 1
    Prohibition 3
    Moonshining in Virginia 4
    Virginia Alcoholic Beverage Control 5

Chapter II:
How to Distill Alcohol 7
    Basic Distillation Process 9
    "The Recipe" 9
    Still Types 10
    Locating a Still 11
    A Filthy Brew 12

Chapter III:
Operation: Cat and Mouse 15
    Duntons Millpond 17
    Mama's Stolen Jam 20
    Up, Up, and Away 21
    A Snowy Day 23
    Barking Dog 24
    Too Drunk to Run 25
    No-Tell Motel 26
    No Turkey this Thanksgiving 27

Antique Shop Capers	28
State Fair	30
Sell and Tell	31
Unlucky 28	31
Over the Top	33
Stuck in the Mud	34
Cat and Mouse	34
Boom Boom	35
Whistle Blower	36
Full Moon	37
Santa Claus	37
No-Plea Indian	39
Another Miserable Night	39
Lost	40
Day Workers	41
Christmas Money	42
Trick or Treat	42
Chicken House	43
Kitchen Caper	44
No Show	44
Grinning Them Down	45
Jailhouse Heist	47
Ow, I Shot Myself!	48
Minnie's Pool Hall	49
Watermelon Man	50
One Under the Bed	55
Drove into the Still	57

    Camp 17 59

    Drinking Swamp 61

    The Brass Band 62

    Nervous Bea 62

    A Snowy Day on Dragon Run 63

    Old Man in King George 64

    Daddy's Little Girl 64

    County Official 65

    Identical Twins 66

    Finders, Keepers 67

    State Record 67

    Woody is My Man 69

    Moonshiner Disguise 70

    Someone Spiked the Iced Tea 71

    Barn Party 72

    Fox and Hounds 74

    Pepsi-Cola Caper 75

    Drunk Coon 76

    Birthday Suit 77

    School Bus Story 77

    Icehouse 78

    About Chauffeur 79

Conclusion 81

Glossary 83

Appendix 85

References 119

Preface

Many people think moonshining takes place primarily in mountainous regions, but my thirty-five-year career as a Virginia Alcoholic Beverage Control (**ABC**) agent shows that the illegal business of distilling liquor is *Not Necessarily in Them Thar Hills*. Each story has factual information, characters long remembered, and slight embellishment as I have spent decades retelling them over and over. And so my story begins.

Introduction

Growing up in Tappahannock, Virginia, I wanted nothing more than to be a policeman. In 1954, I was drafted by the US Army and was stationed for two years in Japan during the Korean conflict. I returned home after my military duty and later earned a degree in law enforcement. My work with the Virginia Alcoholic Beverage Control (ABC), the state equivalent of the Federal Bureau of Alcohol, Tobacco, and Firearms (**ATF**), was a rich, fun, and rewarding career.

In my thirty-eight years with the Virginia ABC, I spent nearly two decades in the enforcement division working stills before becoming an agent and then special agent in charge engaged in regulatory work. Much of my efforts focused on fighting the illegal industry of bootlegging—the illegal manufacture, distribution, or transportation of liquor.

Early in my career, I witnessed the deeply entrenched practice of bootlegging in many rural areas of Virginia where families would teach the younger generation how to run a still and profit from the sale of homemade whiskey. Many of these people believed that moonshining wasn't truly a crime but rather a long-standing way of life that no authority had the right to question. Getting caught was a cat-and-mouse game moonshiners played with local law enforcement.

No two days were the same. My work involved everything

from locating stills and tracking the illegal transportation of alcohol to raiding **nip joints** and performing undercover work throughout the state of Virginia. On any given day, I would make time to call on informants, walk miles into the woods in search of a still, check the status of the **mash** at a still to see when it would be ready to run, and sleep on the ground overnight when a bust looked imminent. After arrests were made, small stills were destroyed by chopping up the operation with axes while large ones were eliminated with explosives. It was important to destroy the equipment so that moonshiners would find it difficult to continue the illegal act. However, we often left one remaining barrel for job security. In a month, I sometimes discovered up to five stills, made fifteen to twenty arrests, and seized a handful of vehicles. There were many occasions when large raids lasted a few days with hundreds of arrests. I figure that over my career lifetime, I took part in between three hundred and five hundred raids.

Though my job was fraught with danger, I fared very well. I remained mostly unharmed over the years, even after being shot at while on a stakeout at a liquor store. That was arguably my closest call. All other injuries I sustained were minor, and almost all happened during car accidents I was involved in while chasing moonshiners.

I supervised ABC enforcement activities in eight Virginia counties: Westmoreland, Northumberland, Lancaster, Richmond, King George, Essex, King and Queen, and Middlesex. Even though my territory was considered a two-man post and I shared many of my experiences with a number of different partners, I often worked alone. I have reason to believe that I earned the respect of many bootleggers as a worthy opponent. Some moonshiners I have known all my life, and many I have arrested multiple times. One of them even published a story recounting tales of making whiskey in my shadow of legal vigilance. I fondly recall a man who once told me, "It's getting so a guy can't make a dishonest living."

I retired in 1991, and as a testament to the love I had for my job, I had accumulated four thousand unused hours of sick leave. I pause only briefly to say that I never had a day when I didn't look forward to going to work.

I am now a bailiff with the Essex County sheriff's office and see some violators that I put behind bars years ago who are appearing in court on other charges. Believe it or not, I can call them my friends even to this day. Before I recount the many tales of chasing moonshiners and dissect the daily reports from my days as an ABC agent, it is important to first understand the history of Prohibition, how bootlegging came to be, and why the ABC Board was and is a necessary enforcement entity. This context sets the stage for my work *Not Necessarily in Them Thar Hills*.

Chapter I

The History of Prohibition, Moonshining, and Virginia ABC

Chapter I: The History of Prohibition, Moonshining, and Virginia ABC

Prohibition

Prohibition was the period from 1919 to 1933 in the United States during which the manufacture, transportation, import, export, and sale of alcoholic beverages were restricted or illegal. Initially a movement to warn Americans of the dangers of alcohol and to convince them to stop drinking, advocates of temperance later campaigned to change the laws to restrict and abolish the sale of liquor. There was great concern that consumption was spreading and was harmful to society, so the government got involved. It was believed that once license to do business was removed from the liquor traffic, the churches and reform organizations would be able to persuade Americans to give up drinking and eventually transition to a sober nation. The Eighteenth Amendment issued this most extreme regulatory liquor law. Although the amendment's ratification was certified on January 16, 1919, it didn't actually take effect until January 17, 1920.

Over the next fourteen years, the illicit manufacture and smuggling of liquor sprang up with such rapidity that authorities were unable to keep up. Plus, the cost of enforcing Prohibition was high, and the lack of tax revenues on alcohol affected government funds. It was only a matter of time before the Twenty-First Amendment repealed nationwide Prohibition and gave states the right to restrict or ban the purchase and sale of alcohol. In October 1933, Virginia citizens voted to implement a liquor control plan.

Moonshining in Virginia

The prohibition of alcohol presented a profitable opportunity for organized crime to take over the importation, manufacture, and distribution of alcoholic beverages. It became a lucrative **moonshine** market when liquor was no longer legally available.

Once the Twenty-First Amendment was passed, people still found it easier and cheaper either to produce and sell moonshine themselves or to support local shiners. With the sale of tax-paid alcohol now legal, moonshiners were committing tax fraud by distilling and selling tax-free liquor. At one point, it was estimated that one bottle of moonshine was consumed for every fifteen bottles of legal spirits. Thus, the cheap but vile product sold by tax evaders continued to provide enormous profits.

Known as the Moonshine Belt, twelve states in the Southeast, including Virginia, produced the bulk of moonshine. Because of Virginia's diverse terrain, moonshining took place in the mountains along its western border and across the flatlands of the state all the way to the coast. Along the Rappahannock River, moonshiners located in the Middle Peninsula and Northern Neck of Virginia had to be especially crafty in order to disguise their illegal operations. Stills were carefully placed miles away from highways, using rural resources to hide their location.

Moonshine earned a number of monikers, depending on the geographic location and dialect. Common terms used in Virginia include hooch, devil's brew, white mule, rotgut, bootleg, firewater, and white lightning.

Virginia Alcoholic Beverage Control

As a result of the Twenty-First Amendment, the Virginia ABC was formed on March 7, 1934, to operate as a public safety agency with law enforcement responsibilities, a major source of revenue for the commonwealth, and an efficient retail business. The Virginia ABC's primary role was to control the distribution of alcoholic beverages, and it relied on its employees to achieve high standards of organizational excellence in achieving this mission.

Soon after the establishment of the state-level agency whose national equivalent is the Federal Bureau of Alcohol, Tobacco, and Firearms (ATF), the first Virginia ABC store opened in Richmond. In 1936, ABC agents were granted full police powers statewide. Two years later, Thomas Massie Gravely was shot while raiding a still and became the first ABC agent killed in the line of duty. In 1952, the ABC Bureau of Law Enforcement purchased unmarked cars, aircraft, and radio equipment to increase surveillance of illegal stills. And in 1958, Robert Floyd Watkins joined the agency.

Chapter II

How to Distill Alcohol

Chapter II: How to Distill Alcohol

Basic Distillation Process

A simple distillation apparatus consists of three parts: a container with a thermometer and an outlet tube from which the vapor is emitted, a container with coiled condensing tubes or "**worms**" (one inside the other), and a vessel to collect the condensed vapor. The mash, a combination of grain, sugar, and water, undergoes the **fermentation** process by being heated in the first container until vaporized, then cooled by the condenser and run off into the receiving vessel. The apparatus used in this process is called the still.

Sometimes, an additional container is used in the distillation process. This container is called the **thumper** or the **doubler**. Its primary function is to collect the mash overflow that hasn't yet turned into vapor and prevent the moonshine from becoming cloudy.

"The Recipe"

1. One bag of grain corn, chicken feed, or hog feed
2. Keep warm and it will soon start to work
3. After it stops working put it in the still to cook.
4. When it starts to boil, keep it below 212 degrees.
5. When it comes out the end of the coil put the jug under the condenser spout and collect the liquid.

6. Cut the first gallon with water as it runs about 120 proof.
7. Add burnt sugar or raisins if you need color.

I read somewhere that if you are not sure it is good stuff, give it to your friend. If he survives, drink some yourself.

- Original recipe from an old moonshiner (guaranteed a fight to a pint)

Still Types

Across my territory in Virginia, each area and sometimes each moonshining family used a different type of still and usually set the operation up differently as well.

Moonshiners in Westmoreland County and other parts of the Northern Neck used small copper pots as stills, anywhere from forty to fifty gallons, and a cooling device known as the worm that was either made of a copper coil or a copper device that looked like a car muffler but functioned exactly like the coil. This car muffler look-alike was most prominent in the White Oak Swamp area.

King and Queen County had larger stills, usually made of steel, and used truck radiators as condensers. They also had upright **boilers**, sometimes ten feet tall. If the still was big enough and created hundreds of gallons of mash, moonshiners would lay several sections of copper pipe in a part of the swamp that had been dammed. This device was known as a **lay worm**. One end of the pipe would connect to the still while the other end pushed through the dam to continuously collect water.

In Essex County, moonshiners had fifty-five-gallon steel barrels filled with water that were called boilers. The boilers sent steam into a fifty-five-gallon wooden barrel filled with mash, then into another wooden barrel called the doubler, and finally into a coiled condenser. One of my favorite moonshiners in Essex had a recognizable **rig** because he always hung his workpants on the connecting pipe between the boiler and the still. Other moonshiners' trademarks cannot be retold.

Locating a Still

There are a number of ways to locate a still. Because moonshiners were very good at camouflaging their stills, I often searched for paths or traffic patterns leading to a still. Moonshiners needed a way to transport their product and could do so by foot, by automobile, or sometimes by boat. I routinely checked the traffic of all three kinds and sometimes did so by air. The state of Virginia owned two aircraft that were accessible by the ABC enforcement division to search for stills in woods, fields, and ponds. Many of my discoveries were made this way.

The best sources of information were my informants, so I made sure to contact them on a regular basis. Bootleggers turned on each other from time to time in order to cut down on competition or for vengeance. It was good for me to check in often and to keep a close eye on them.

A Filthy Brew

Because of the outdoor, backwoods environment where moonshiners were forced to distill liquor in an attempt to do so secretively, sanitation was rarely a consideration. It wasn't uncommon to find additional ingredients in the mash during still raids. In many instances, a distillery's end product was contaminated with rats, maggots, and Clorox, producing a foul odor and rancid moonshine. Some moonshiners even added **lye** to their mash to speed the fermenting process. Operations were not only dirty but also dangerous.

Mash Boxes

Eventually, moonshine's health hazards became public knowledge. The US Food and Drug Administration reported moonshine as a serious health menace because of the amount of lead substances or other hazardous toxic chemicals in it. More than one thousand micrograms of lead salts per liter is considered poisonous, and it was confirmed by laboratory tests that the greater proportion of all moonshine seized surpassed that threshold. Blindness, heart damage, muscle weakness, impairment of kidney function, brain damage, paralysis, or death was often the high price paid by consumers of such a product. With alcohol production largely in the hands of criminals and unregulated, clandestine home manufacturers, the quality of product varied widely, and the risk for a deadly drink was high.

Chapter III

Operation: Cat and Mouse

Chapter III: Operation: Cat and Mouse

In my lifetime, I arrested more moonshiners than I care to remember, but I always enjoyed the hunt, the chase, and now, the stories. Contrary to the origin of the word "moonshine" (meaning "at night"), I caught 75 percent of my violators during daylight. They were not ashamed of what they were doing. They were just trying to make a living. Just like you and me. They weren't bad people, but it was my job to see that they made as little moonshine as possible. It was literally a game of cat and mouse. I was the cat, and the moonshiners were the mice. In the pages that follow are a small sample of the daily events I encountered as an agent. The stories are written using my own words, with my personal tone and include occasional swearing. This is how it was. This is how I wanted it written. I hope you enjoy my collection of bootleg stories.

Duntons Millpond

I had a friend who was a farmer in Lancaster County. He paid me a visit one day and told me that he thought something was going on near Duntons Millpond. I went to check out the site later that day with my partner, Mickey Amos, and found the nicest, most beautiful still I had ever laid eyes on. It was a copper still with ten barrels of mash. We checked the mash and determined it would be ready to run in a day or two. We then looked up the pathway and saw a man with a gun headed in our direction. I drew my gun immediately in order to protect myself, but it turned out to only be a hunter who had permission from the landowner, my farmer friend, to hunt on his property. We let him go but told him that if he breathed a word about the still, we would gladly pay him a visit. He told my friend later that he was so scared to death that he didn't even tell his wife.

Still in Lancaster County

Upon our return the next day, we saw that the still was in full operation and being run by a moonshiner I had come to know very well and his brother. The moonshiner's name was JT, and I had arrested him many times. He, in fact, is the one who gave me my first nickname, Wats. He called me this because he had trouble pronouncing my last name, Watkins, and because it was catchy.

I remember JT's first arrest. It was for two barrels of mash. I told him then that if he was going to bootleg, he might as well bootleg more barrels at one time because it was too much trouble to only bother with the two. There was another time not long after his first arrest when I raided another of his rigs and seized a pistol from him. I turned the gun over to the sheriff, like we were supposed to. This pistol must have had some sentimental value or at least meant a lot to JT because he wanted the gun back bad enough that he asked the sheriff himself for it. The sheriff told him that he had given the gun back to me, which was a lie. The truth was that he had given it to a deputy. JT learned of the truth over time and hated that dishonest sheriff until the day he died.

While I was talking to JT during this particular arrest, I heard a noise from behind and turned to see JT's brother jumping into the pond. He did this so fast that he got away from us. My partner took JT to the jail so that he, too, wouldn't get away, while I drove his vehicle to the sheriff's office. When JT was released from jail the next day, he stole the car back from the sheriff's lot. Payback.

Believe it or not, JT and I became friends even though I had arrested him many times. Back in those days, it wasn't uncommon for a bootlegger to help out an agent in need or vice versa. We understood that it was a game of cat and mouse. They were going to make whiskey, and we were going to do what we had to do to see that justice prevailed. It was nothing more than that. There were no hard feelings.

Mama's Stolen Jam

I picked up one of my informants on the pretense of him showing me where a still was located in the upper end of Essex County. Upon his directions, I pulled into a dirt lane leading to a house. He pointed out the house and told me that a small still was located behind the dwelling. Just as I was backing out of the lane, a car came in behind me. The informer proceeded to lie down on the floor of my state car knowing that if someone saw him, his life would not be worth a plug nickel. I got out of the car, and the other car backed up into the field next to the road.

Boxes of Mason Jars

I recognized the operator as a known moonshiner in the area. The violator was about to run me down. I pulled out my .38 revolver and told him, "You had better cut the engine off, or I will blow the windshield out." The bootlegger got out of the vehicle and said to me, "Damn, Mr. Watkins, I believe you were going to shoot me." My statement to him in return was, "You can count on it." Upon checking the vehicle, I found 480 pounds of sugar and six cases of jars. I told him he had two choices: to unload the sugar and jars or to go downtown with me. He did not realize that I didn't have anything to charge him with at the time since it is perfectly legal to possess sugar and jars in any quantity. Regardless, he unloaded everything onto the side of the road and spun wheels exiting the scene.

That night he called the sheriff, claiming that someone had hijacked his vehicle and stolen the sugar and jars that he was taking to his mother to can jam. The moonshiner never got his products back. Instead, I gave the sugar to a man who had beehives so he could feed his bees in the winter.

Up, Up, and Away

We located a stash of raw materials outside of Richmond, Virginia, where one of the big-time bootleggers was storing his sugar and jars. We put one agent on the ground to observe the stash while I was on standby at Hanover Airport with a state-assigned aircraft, waiting for the call that the violators had loaded their supplies. I got the call that they were loading the supplies and preparing for transport, so we lifted into the air and took off in the direction of the stash. Still waiting for word that the supply was in motion, we killed time circling Byrd Airport, which was closer to the stash. During this time, we were constantly being instructed by the airport tower to increase or lower altitudes because of landings into the airport, and our nerves were on an all-time high.

Lucky for us, we finally got word that the loaded product was now being transported by two vehicles traveling one behind the other. In many cases, cars would travel separately and make it much more difficult for us to keep up with the supply. We followed the violators into the night as they ran us around Robin Hood's barn. As soon as I saw the bootleggers cross the bridge at West Point and enter into my territory, King and Queen County, I knew exactly where we were and the likely destination. The violators turned off the lights on their vehicles upon arriving at the location of the still, and, with the map in my lap, I was able to pinpoint its exact coordinates.

We went to the still the next morning, and it was in full operation. I literally crawled into the middle of the mash boxes without any of the violators seeing me and witnessed up close and in person their offense. This was a large operation with four thousand gallons of mash and a five-hundred-gallon still alongside an upright boiler. Needless to say, the three violators were arrested and taken to trial. During the trial, the court took the jury down to the still site to observe the location. This was the only time that I had this happen. All were convicted of illegal manufacture and given six months in jail to be served.

A Snowy Day

I received a call from an unknown informant concerning a still located behind his house. The man said that his wife and daughter had come across the still while fetching water at the stream behind their house. He went on to tell me that they were also being harassed by the still operators and had had enough. Later that evening, I visited the man at his humble house located in Westmoreland County near the King George County line. The house that the man lived in had no running water or any other modern-day convenience. From the outside, it looked like an abandoned, dilapidated shack. The siding had been ripped from the house and was being burned for warmth. On the inside, the family of five or more occupied only one room with a pile of rags in one corner of the room used as a bed.

It was snowing at the time. The man stepped outside to show me the way to the still but had no shoes on. I asked him, "Aren't you going to put on some shoes?" He said, "If I had some, I would put them on." Out we went, me with boots on and him without. The rig had a nice fifty-gallon copper still and four hundred gallons of mash. I tasted the mash and determined that it would be ready to run the next day.

Upon arriving at the site the morning after, my partner and I saw two vehicles parked on the woods road just before a broken-down bridge. We then headed into the woods toward the still and could hear activity. The moonshiners' chatter, the roaring of the gas burner, the thumping of the thumper, and the smell of the mash had my adrenaline pumping. The still was fired up and running when we got there, with three violators hard at work. My partner and I split up. He ran after one in the woods while I quickly grabbed the other two and cuffed them together before they knew what hit them. After the arrests, we chopped up the distillery and seized the two vehicles. When we came out of the woods, the county sheriff was waiting for us. He had been looking for the two violators we had cuffed together, who turned out to be brothers who had beaten a man to death with a baseball bat. Never realizing I had two murderers on my hands, I said to myself, "What a lucky day!"

Barking Dog

I had information on a still near Oak Grove in Westmoreland County. I walked up behind the house in question, and from my vantage point, I could see the still and mash box located in an outbuilding behind the main dwelling. There was a dog chained next to the outbuilding that kept barking, which prevented me from getting close enough to see if there was mash in the mash box. After several failed attempts at approaching the rig unnoticed, I realized that I first needed to come up with a plan for how to keep the dog quiet.

The next day, I decided to go to the local veterinarian to inquire about the possibility of getting something to put the dog to sleep for a short time so I could check out things. The vet asked how much the dog weighed, and I told him about forty pounds. I did not want to kill the dog, but just impose a quick nap. I went back to check on the still one last time before taking such a drastic measure only to find that dog was as quiet as a mouse. Although I found this to be strange, I was able to walk up to the site with no problem except to find that the still was gone. The dog was smarter than I thought!

Still in a barn in Westmoreland County

Too Drunk to Run

I received a call from a farmer in Essex County who thought something was going on at the lower part of his farm. I went down to the swamp near the place he had described and found a small copper still with only one barrel of mash. The still was a square copper still—the only square one I had seen—but it was not yet in operation.

When I revisited the site two days later, there was a man sitting down holding a jar with good old moonshine going into it. His entire run that day was one quart, and he had drank half of that himself. I walked right up to the perpetrator and wished him a good morning. He never said a word in return and was too drunk to run. It was the easiest arrest I ever had, except that he smelled so badly of body odor on the way to the jail that I had to drive with the windows down.

No-Tell Motel

I located a still in King George County behind a truck stop on Route 301. The truck stop was next door to a small motel. A federal officer that I was working with at the time and I rented a room where we had a view of the back of the truck stop. Assuming we had a long wait on our hands, we went to the grocery store to get some provisions to hold us over.

While observing the still site, we would watch the truck-stop owner's son get off the bus every day after school. The boy, who was about fourteen years of age, would run around the junkyard behind the motel and chase chickens. In perfect view from our motel window, we would watch him catch the chickens, throw them in a wrecked car, and literally ring their necks until dead. Although entertaining, this boy was crazy. I told the ATF agent that I was going to kill that little son of bitch myself once we finally raided the still down the hill.

Over the course of our two days in the motel, we also observed two men who worked and lived at the truck stop going to and from the still. We would take turns following them into the woods until we felt the time was right to raid. Finally, the agent and I raided the still from different directions. The violator that I arrested had his shirt off and was covered with hair. It was like grabbing a gorilla.

We took the bootleggers back up to the truck stop to see if they had any other evidence of moonshining on the property. Much to our surprise, we found another still under construction in the building. Talk about a two-for-one.

No Turkey this Thanksgiving

Oftentimes we worked with other local law enforcement officers, including game wardens. On this one occasion, my partner Gordon Birkett and I were working with the game warden in Essex County. He was checking on hunters spotlighting deer. It happened to be Thanksgiving Eve. While we were out, we also checked on an area where still operations were known to be. On a winding road in the upper end of the county, we met a vehicle that we believed to be hauling moonshine. It was a 1958 Buick. My partner was driving, I was riding shotgun and the game warden was in the backseat. We turned around and attempted to catch up with the speeding vehicle, but the back road had just been tarred and the gravel was loose. At a high rate of speed, we lost control, hit several trees, and were thrown out of the vehicle into the middle of the road. The car was totaled, but I managed to find the radio and report the accident with a small glimmer of hope that someone would respond. Much to my surprise, the dispatcher in Richmond answered on the first call. This was unexpected, not only because of the poor condition of the car but because it was 1:00 a.m. on Thanksgiving morning.

I only suffered minor injuries, but my partner was on the critical list for quite some time. While he was still hospitalized, I raided a still near where we had wrecked, and one of the violators I arrested was the driver of the vehicle that we had been chasing that ominous night. He told me he had twenty-eight cases of moonshine in the car the night of the accident and that he started to pull over and wait for us because he knew he could not outrun us. He swore that had he known that we had wrecked he would have come back and helped us. And he would have, too. Back in those days things were different.

Antique Shop Capers

One afternoon on his way to a fishing trip in the Northern Neck, my director of the enforcement division, John Wright, stopped at an antique shop in Northumberland County. Low and behold, there was a copper still sitting on the shelf. Because it is illegal to possess a functioning still in the state of Virginia without a license, and because he was on vacation, he called me to pay a visit to the shop owner. I went over to the antique shop, located in Callao, and confronted the lady in charge. I requested to see the license required for a distillery, and, of course, she did not have one. When I seized the still, she told me that her husband would have shot me if he had been there. I told her that it was a good thing he wasn't, because it was probable that I might have shot him instead. She hated me until her dying day.

Still in Essex County

In a similar instance, I received a call from a federal agent in Maryland who had observed an antique dealer from Virginia purchase a copper still at an auction he attended. The antique shop just happened to be located right across the street from my office at the sheriff's department in Essex County. I went across the street to the antique shop and confronted the owner about the still. He denied that he had the still. I told him, "Don't make me get a search warrant." He reluctantly took me down in the basement, and there sat the prettiest six-foot-tall copper still. I asked him where the cap was to the top, and he told me that no such cap existed. Once again I said, "Don't make me get a search warrant." He gave me the cap, which was stashed over in the corner. And so, another enemy was made in the antique world that day.

State Fair

Every year around September, the State Fair comes to Richmond. Each state agency had a booth with items on display and information. Every agent with the enforcement division had to pull his turn manning the booth. While I was on duty, an old-timer came into the booth, which had two or three copper stills and some models of other stills. The older man was looking at one of the models. I was just standing around with a coat and tie on, not saying anything. The old man said to me, "That is a nice setup." I responded, "Yes, that is a nice one." Without thinking, he then said, "My still is not as big as that one." The old-timer looked up from the display and asked, "Who are you?" I told him that I was an agent with the ABC Board. The old-timer replied, "It appears that I am talking to the wrong man." Just kidding, I then asked him, "Where did you say you lived?" He just walked away.

Sell and Tell

Sometimes I would receive information from operators of old country stores that sold sugar and jars. On one occasion, I obtained information from a store owner about a known violator who was going to pick up a large quantity of sugar. I made arrangements to get an aircraft up in the air over the store while I took a vantage point in a barn located across the road. I was watching them load the sugar into a vehicle through binoculars as the airplane circled overhead. The store owner was helping the violators move the product and kept looking over in my direction to see if I was witnessing the crime. After awhile, the vehicle was finally loaded and ready for transport. The agent in the plane followed the vehicle then called me on the radio to give me its location once it had parked. We watched the vehicle for two days, but it never moved. I guess they smelled a rat. Maybe it was the aircraft or maybe it was the jittery store owner who glanced periodically over my way and acted suspicious. These things I'm not sure of, but it certainly didn't work to our favor this time.

Unlucky 28

While checking back roads in the upper end of Essex County, my partner and I located twenty-eight cases of moonshine down a woods road. The cases were covered with a canvas to camouflage them from trespassers. We knew that the violators would not leave the stash for long, so we hid the state car down the woods road and found a comfortable spot on the ground near the twenty-eight cases to wait. We would "hurry up and wait" a lot. While playing the waiting game, I spent time mastering the art of a good catnap, playing many a game of hearts, and having my patience tested plenty.

Finally, a car came just before dark. One of the violators got out of the car to direct the driver who was backing up to the cases of whiskey. I grabbed the driver by the neck through the open window, and he hit the gas in an attempt to escape. As the car spun wheels, the violator on the ground dove through the window on the other side and into the car. The car got away and left me covered from head to toe in mud. I shot at the suspects' vehicle and hit it five times before it made a sharp turn about twenty feet away. Once the car was no longer in sight, I ran back to my state car that my partner had uncovered from its disguise of tree branches and began to chase after them. We caught up to the vehicle in time to see the violators wreck it and run from the car. Both men got away. As for the vehicle, it contained no moonshine. It was a good thing I did not injure anybody when I shot because I didn't have anything to charge anyone with. We had the vehicle towed to the sheriff's office, and it sat outside for two weeks without anyone claiming it. I was later contacted by the violator, who told me that I had basically taken $750 right out of his pocket the night of the incident. He and his partner had already sold the whiskey and were planning to receive payment for delivery that night.

Over the Top

I located a nice still in King and Queen County. I checked the mash and determined from the taste of it that the still was ready to run soon. My partner and I went to the still the next day to find that it was in full operation. When we raided the still, I observed three violators. All three took flight! I ran one down and cuffed him to a small pine tree. My partner caught one while I managed to chase down and capture the third. When I got back to the first violator that I had cuffed to the tree, he was halfway up the trunk, breaking limbs as he went. He told me, "Mr. Watkins, if I had had five more minutes I would have been over the top." We destroyed the still and took the violators to jail. One of the violators asked me if I would take twenty dollars to his wife so she could buy groceries. I told him that I would and headed for their house about thirty miles away. Halfway there, I saw her headed in the opposite direction and flagged down her vehicle. I informed her that I had just caught her husband at the still and that he was in jail. She was mad as hell. I also told her about the twenty dollars. She demanded that I hand it over, but I told her that she first needed to sign a receipt for it. She was adamant that she wasn't going to sign anything, but she did so reluctantly on the back of an envelope retrieved from the glove box once she learned that she wasn't getting her money without it. I see this woman quite often these days, and she gives me a hug each time. We are now friends. She's obviously had a change of heart. I guess time heals all.

Stuck in the Mud

While checking an area that we received information on in the upper end of Essex County, my partner and I were investigating car tracks around the edge of a field. It had just rained that day, and we got stuck in the mud up to the frame of the state car. Low and behold, here came a well-known moonshiner who helped us get out of the mud. This moonshiner was the one we believed to be connected to the still we were in search of. Later that day, we located his still and chopped it up. When we saw him a day or two afterward, he asked us, "I just want to ask you one thing. Did you chop my still before I helped you get out of the mud or after?" The reply was "After!" He said, "Well, that's all right then."

Cat and Mouse

I ran up on a known moonshiner while checking back roads in the upper end of Essex County. His car looked like it was heavy in the back end. I gave chase on the back road, which was narrow and crooked as a snake. After about five miles of high-speed pursuit, he pulled over. I asked him if I could take a look in his trunk, and he obliged. When he opened the trunk, it was full of nothing but storm windows and other junk! I asked him why he took off, and he said, "I just wanted to see how fast you could drive, Mr. Watkins." We both had a good laugh. Another day of cat and mouse!

Boom Boom

I got a call from a big landowner in King and Queen County about a still located on his property. In this case, the still was located directly behind a house, but we had to walk one or two miles around so that we entered from the back without being detected. This was a large 250-gallon still, with a 200-gallon boiler and about 2,000 gallons of mash. To show you how clever these moonshiners were, they would gain access to the still by removing a woodpile at the end of the driveway to clear the path then cover their tracks piece by piece each time.

Still in King and Queen County

We ended up spending the night since the still was not quite ready to run. While we were sleeping early the next morning, one of the violators was scoping out the area and inadvertently stumbled upon us. Realizing who we were, he took off like a bat out of hell. Because we felt sure that our cover had been blown, we went in and wired the still with dynamite. The still was very close to the house. When we blew the still, mash rained down on the house, along with other debris. We woke up the whole neighborhood that day!

Whistle-Blower

My partner and I were checking a still located in Essex County one afternoon, enjoying a shaded walk around the edge of a field, when we saw a man out of the corner of our eye take off running in the opposite direction of where we believed the still to be. Rather than chase the man, we continued toward the possible still site. When we proved ourselves right and reached the site, another two men took off running. I chased one of the men, who had gained quite a jump on me and was already about twenty-five yards away. There was thick underbrush, and I could no longer see or hear him up ahead. I knew this meant that he had laid down somewhere and was hiding from me. I walked up to a fallen tree only a few steps ahead, and there he was, lying on his back with a corncob pipe in his mouth. He was a known violator. I had caught him many times. He said to me, "Damn you, got me again." It turns out that the man we saw running in the edge of the field before the raid was the still's watchman. This man had a whistle in his pocket to alert his fellow moonshiners of trespassers or trouble, but he got so scared by our presence that he forgot to blow the whistle.

Full Moon

After discovering a small still in the upper end of Essex County, I spent many days sneaking back and forth from the site in an attempt to catch the moonshiners in the act. The site was set up on top of an old site that I had destroyed years before, so I was very familiar with the territory. Upon checking on the still, I would find empty mash barrels one day and a recently run still the next. It seemed like I had just missed them every time. I made my own pathway to the still in the back that was used even more than the violators' trail in the front. I fooled with that still for weeks, unable to think about anything else and hoping to finally catch those clever violators. I woke up one night and there was a full moon, just bright as day. I said to myself, "I bet he is going to run that still tonight." The thought took me out of bed and to the site. I walked right up to that still, and in no time at all I had the violator in cuffs and placed in jail, and I went back home to sleep.

Santa Claus

I was on the way to the Richmond office, which fellow agents and I often visited for mandatory meetings, to pick up supplies, or to cross-reference information. The game warden from King and Queen County called me while I was en route to say that he had seen some activity in a cow pasture near the Mattaponi River. My partner and I followed the lead while it was hot. We went across two big fields and through two gates then stopped the car as soon as we could smell mash. We hopped out of the

Still in King and Queen County

As we approached, we could hear the still running and someone making a noise down by the river. The violators had put up a barbed-wire fence around the still to keep the cows out. My partner went toward the river while I ducked under the fence. From my vantage point, I could see that the still was in full operation. The still had ten four-hundred-gallon mash boxes all mashed in. There were two men standing near the upright boiler, one eating a can of potted meat. I ran in and arrested the two of them, slapping handcuffs on both. Down by the river, my partner arrested the other, who was building four more mash boxes. It turns out that all three violators were big-time bootleggers. The owner of the still was the one building the mash boxes. I asked him for his name, and I could not believe his response. I had heard of this man all my life and drawn a picture of him in my mind as a big, tough, untouchable man. Much to my surprise, he looked like a little old Santa Claus. He got jail time along with the other two and served it as a trustee at lockup. At that time, prisoners were fed out of the kitchen, but they were left to starve when the jailer ran off with some woman. Santa Claus took care of everyone, a characteristic also reminiscent of Saint Nick. Because of that, his time was suspended.

No-Plea Indian

Lloyds is a crossroad just west of Loretta in the upper end of Essex County. I found a small still in this area that was a family operation. Upon raiding the still, I arrested one young man and an older one with his leg in a cast and on crutches. Bootleggers on crutches were the kind that I liked: easy to catch. When I went to court with him, the judge asked him if he wanted to plead guilty or not guilty. The violator said, "Well, Judge, to tell you the truth, I was just visiting." The judge asked one more time, trying to control his temper, "Are you guilty or not guilty." Same answer. The judge never did get a plea, but after due conversation, he entered a not guilty plea for him. He was convicted of illegal manufacture and was given a suspended sentence. This man was a Rappahannock Indian, and I arrested many of his family members.

Another Miserable Night

I received information on a large still far back in the woods in Essex County. Once I located the still myself, I immediately noticed that it was mashed in but that the mash was about to "go back," a common term in the bootlegging business. In other words, the mash was about to turn sour. I came back to spend the night and keep a watchful eye over the rig. I had a federal officer with me that night, and we both thought that the mosquitoes would eat us alive! We were near an airport. As the hours passed, I began to notice that the sound of the airplanes' engines as they approached would chase the mosquitoes away but that they would come back when the sound faded. Needless to say, the constant swatting at mosquitoes and buzzing of airplane engines kept me wide awake all night. Once dawn broke the next morning and it was evident that the violators were not going to return anytime soon, the federal officer and I destroyed the still with TNT and left four thousand gallons of mash dripping from the treetops. On the car ride home, he asked me if I had noticed that very same correlation between the mosquitoes and the engines. Apparently, he didn't get much sleep either.

Lost

No one wants to admit that he is lost, but when you are working the woods and walking for miles in heavy timberland, you do just that. You get lost. It was a standing joke: I never got lost, just turned around. One time I got turned around after going in to check on a still. It had started to rain and a storm was fast approaching. I was not paying too much attention to where I was going because I was just trying to get back to the state car before the storm hit. The area I was walking in is known as White Oak Swamp. There are no known landmarks, just swamp and water. I found a lot of stills in those woods. If I could not find one before lunchtime, it was a slow day. En route, I was not surprised to walk up on another still that was not in operation at the time. I made a mental note of its location, but quickly moved on, still trying to find my way. After walking for quite a long time, I came up on a hard-surfaced road and literally had no idea which road it was. A vehicle stopped and took me back to my car. Come to find out, I had walked about four miles. I had difficulty finding the still that I had walked up on the second time, too. Turned around again.

Day Workers

There are places in Richmond City where unemployed people gather to look for work. These people would do just about anything for a little bit of money and for no defined period of time. Still operators would often stop by one of these places to find the hopeful workers standing around a steel barrel with fire in it to keep them warm. The still operator would ask if anyone wanted a week's worth of work. The first to reply "yes" were then taken into the woods and dropped off. Their job would be to help operate the still and the workers were paid per box of mash. Most of the time, they would live in a tent with little to no means. When we would raid the still and arrest these people, they had no idea where they were or who their employer was. This was a good thing for the violators. The people arrested could not give us any information.

Christmas Money

Everyone knew that the price of copper was high in the 1960s and 1970s. Copper scrap was sixty-five cents a pound. This was a good price back then. When we chopped up a still, we sometimes saved the copper and sold it to a junk dealer in West Point. We kind of kept it a secret since we did not know if the state of Virginia would frown on such a thing. When we arrived at West Point on one of our trips just before Christmas, we saw another pile of copper in the yard that contained still parts. I asked the dealer, "Where did you get that copper?" He checked the invoice and said that the name of the seller was James Brown. I had a sneaky suspicion that it was one of my cohorts from the Richmond office who had used this fictitious name and must have needed some Christmas money as well. The next day, I passed him in the hallway and said, "How are you doing, James Brown?" He knew exactly what I was talking about. If he had checked *our* invoice, he would have read Mickey Mouse! We both had a good laugh.

Trick or Treat

I located a small still with an ATF agent in Lancaster County behind a house on the Corrotoman River. We went in to check on the still late one night. This particular evening happened to be especially dark and spooky. It was Halloween. We could hear the kids trick-or-treating up at the house. The ATF agent and I were in hopes that the moonshiner would come in since the still was ready to run. We were joking that when he came to run the still, we were going to give him a big scare and say, "Trick or treat." However, he did not run the still that night. We checked the still a couple more times only to find that the violator had finally moved the still. Sometimes you win; sometimes you lose.

Chicken House

I was sitting down at the dinner table one night and the phone rang. The voice on the other end said, "There is a still located in Middlesex County on Route 625 in the little village of Wake." The subject gave me the location and told me, "by the way," that it was located under the chicken house behind the main house! I made a call to an ATF agent and made plans to meet him near Saluda, another small town in Middlesex County. The ATF agent and I went to the location. There was a light on in the dwelling, and there was a forty-five-foot-long chicken house with white leghorn chickens running around all over the place. We climbed over a fence and stumbled into a hog lot. An old mama sow with little pigs did not take too kindly that we were getting too close to her babies! The old sow let out a squeal and made a break toward the ATF officer. You have never seen a man go over a fence as fast as he did. After we got mama pig taken care of, we proceeded to the chicken house. We went into the chicken house, and the floor was covered with wood shavings. In one corner was a potbelly stove with the chimney going up through the roof to keep the chickens warm. We found a trap door, covered in shavings, in the floor. The violators would sweep the shavings back and go down to the still through this door. By covering the trap door back up with the shavings, no one would know a still was operating below. To cover up the smoke that came out of the boiler down at the still, they ran a pipe through the bottom of the stove so the smoke went up the chimney. We discovered that the still was dry and had not been run for some time. We put an ax to the still and the other equipment and called it a night.

Kitchen Caper

I obtained a search warrant after receiving information that a man had a small still in his kitchen in Essex County. The house was raided and a still was found on the stove with one fifty-gallon barrel of mash. After placing the bootlegger under arrest, I asked him to help me slide the barrel of mash to the door so I could pour the mash outside and not mess up his kitchen. The violator told me, "That's not my job. You do it." You guessed it. I chopped the barrel right in the middle of the kitchen. What a mess! Mash was running everywhere. The violator never showed up for court. Last I heard, he went to New Jersey.

No Show

My partner, Gordon Birkett, made a buy from a woman bootlegger in the township of Weems, which is located in Lancaster County. When it came time to come to court, the female violator did not show up. Since I was the arresting officer, the judge ordered that I pick her up and bring her to court that day. He said he had information that she had a gun, had purchased ammo, and was going to shoot that little SOB with the green outfit on, which was me. She lived on the water with a long lane to her house. I had a Virginia state trooper drop me off while he continued down the lane. I went around the back of the house and had the trooper approach from the front. Through the window, I could see the gun lying on the kitchen table. When the trooper knocked on the front door, the violator went to answer it while I snuck in and grabbed the gun. Once she saw who was on the other side of the front door, she turned around and ran back down the hall to retrieve the gun, which I already had in my possession. After a nasty scuffle, I managed to get cuffs on her and bring her before the judge. She was given an unusually lengthy sentence of six months in jail after some unnecessary name-calling directed toward both the judge and me.

Grinning Them Down

My partner and I discovered a still in the upper end of Essex County and determined from the taste of the mash that the still would likely be in operation the next day. Twenty-four hours later, we had someone drop us off along with the sheriff of Essex County about a mile from the site and began our walk excitedly in the direction of the still. It was cold as blue blazes, and everything was frozen.

When we arrived to our destination, we could hear the still running and people talking. Knowing that the sheriff was not fleet of foot, we told him to go down to the swamp, which was covered with ice, and wait. Once he was in position, we raided the still. One violator ran down toward the swamp, and I gave chase while the other, also heading for the swamp, was trying to escape from my partner. The bootlegger that I was chasing crossed over to the other side of the swamp where my partner was running just as his violator crossed over to my side. I shouted to my partner, "You take him and I'll take the other one." My new pursuit had broken through the ice, and the mud had sucked both shoes off of his feet. He was running barefooted until he looked up and saw the sheriff standing with his hands on his hips, just grinning. Well, the violator stopped in his tracks. We told the sheriff, "We knew Davey Crockett could grin the bears down, but we didn't know he was capable of grinning moonshiners down!" We had a good time with that one for a long time.

Still in Essex County

Once arrested, the moonshiners asked us if we would stop at the house where one of them lived so someone would come down to the jail and bond them out. When we drove up in the front yard with the violators in the state car, one of their wives, also barefooted, ran out of the house with a shotgun and shot it up in the air. I told her that it was too late to give the violators a warning shot because we already had them in the back of the car. You have never heard a woman scream and cry as loud in your life!

Jailhouse Heist

From time to time, the enforcement division would have an undercover operation where an agent would come into our assigned territory to make buys. Sometimes, the operation would go on for several months. For quite a while, I had an agent working in my territory making buys in the Haynesville area of Richmond County. When we finally raided a nip joint where he had made his fair share of buys, we seized some three hundred pints of legal whiskey. The violators were buying the alcohol from the Virginia ABC store and reselling it at a higher price. This transaction was popular in rural areas and highly illegal. I stored the whiskey in the evidence room in the sheriff's office in Richmond County for safekeeping until the violators were due in court. When it got close to court time, I went over to the office and recounted the bottles of alcohol to make sure the inventory was listed as I had it on the search warrant. Much to my surprise, we were short fourteen pints of liquor! I got in contact with the sheriff and jokingly said, "You got a little thirsty didn't you, Sheriff?" He had no idea what I was talking about. I continued to tell him that we were short on the whiskey that we'd seized the other night. The sheriff told me to put the whiskey back in the evidence room and to let him do some checking. The next day, I went back over to the sheriff's office, and he and I recounted the pints together. This time, we were seventeen pints short!

As it turned out, the sheriff had two inmates serving time for breaking and entering in the county. During these days, the jailer would stay on the premises overnight. When the jailer would go to bed, the inmates would pick the lock on the cell door, go down the hall to the evidence room, then pick the lock on that door, and take whatever they needed to drink for the night. They would get drunk as hell, break the bottles, and flush them down the toilet. The only way we found out about it was because one of the inmates told on the other. The sheriff charged and convicted both men with stealing whiskey while behind bars. I'm pretty sure that was a first.

Ow, I Shot Myself!

All agents with the Virginia ABC Board were required to qualify on the firing range twice a year. This was a training exercise that we always looked forward to. On one of these occasions, about thirty of us were lined up at the firing range. The range officer gave the command from up in the tower, "Ready on the left, ready on the right, ready on the firing line, commence firing." It was at this time that you were supposed to draw your revolver and start firing at the target. This time was different, however. Just before the officer could spit out his final word, I heard a shot go off, and the agent next to me said, "I think I just shot myself!" I raised my hand as you are instructed to do if there is a problem. The range officer in the tower said over the PA system, "Cease fire," then asked "OK, Watkins, what have you done?" I said that this man next to me had just shot himself and that I could see blood running down his leg. In drawing his revolver from the holster with his finger on the trigger, which you are instructed *not* to do, he shot himself in the rear end. It was quite an embarrassment to him but funny to the rest of the agents! They hauled him off to the emergency room at the local hospital and cleaned him up. He did not hit any bones, just the flesh of his rear end. He returned to the range, none the worse, and caught a hard time from the group.

Minnie's Pool Hall

There was another period of time when I had an undercover agent working in my area, this time making buys from a black lady in King George. She was the proprietor of a place called Minnie's Pool Hall. I gave the agent marked money so that we could retrieve it for evidence to be used in court once she was arrested. After making the exchange, the undercover agent informed me that she had put the money he'd given her down in her brassiere on the left side.

We raided the pool hall with the sheriff of the county and a few other officers not long after. The sheriff told Minnie, "OK, Minnie, give me the roll of money that you have next to your left breast." Minnie said, "I don't know what you are talking about." The sheriff told her, "Don't make me go down in there and get the money." Well, Minnie had breasts big as your head, so I could only imagine the sheriff doing just that and having a difficult time finding the sought-after bills.

After a lot of conversation and denied accusations, Minnie eventually pulled out a wad of crumpled-up bills from which we picked out the marked money. Minnie was convicted in court for selling alcoholic beverages without a license, and her arrest is a memory that I still cannot erase no matter how hard I try.

Watermelon Man

Some of my favorite memories I have from my years as an agent were from when I worked undercover for a few summers as a watermelon man. I worked a **huckster** truck, selling peaches and watermelons in a lot of cities and towns in the state of Virginia, mostly in black areas. If you were white and a stranger, you had to have a reason to be in those parts, and selling watermelons was the ticket! I would make purchases of illegal whiskey then report the transactions to the local officers. When we had the big roundup, another term for raid, I was required to come around and identify the persons I had made the purchases from. Everyone loved the watermelon man until then. The following short stories paint an accurate description of my experience as an undercover agent.

- While working in Blackstone, I would often visit an old bootlegger named Buck. Now old Buck was a good old boy and he and I had become friends. I had purchased whiskey from his wife, his son, and old Buck himself. On one of my visits, Buck saw a man steal a watermelon out of my truck while I was in Buck's house talking to him. Before I knew what had happened, Buck chased the man up the street and made him bring the melon back and put it in my truck. He then threatened to kill him. The day of the roundup, I was at Buck's house when the raiding party came in because of the information I had previously given them. The local officer in charge asked me to identify the people I had purchased from. Feeling a little guilty and with a sliver of hesitation, I pointed out Buck, his wife, and son. Buck was in shock. He had no idea I was who I was and swore, "Damn a watermelon, I will never eat another one."

- I went to a house one afternoon that had previously been pointed out to me by local officers. I walked up the stairs to the house and asked a teenage girl who was sitting on the porch if the lady of the house was in. The girl told me that she was sick in the back bedroom but to go on in. I walked to back bedroom, saw the woman lying in bed, and asked her if she had any whiskey. She pointed at some bags on the table. I asked, "How much for a pint?" She told me one was only five dollars, so I paid her and went out the door. I came back to the house a few days later and asked again if the lady of the house was in. The girl once again replied, "Yea," and asked if I wanted to see her. I followed the girl into the house and there in the parlor was the lady of the house in a coffin. She was dead as hell. That was the only violator I did not arrest when we had the roundup!

- In the same town, I went to the EF Dance Hall to make a purchase. The owner of the dance hall was a female and had a daughter who was crazy as hell, especially with a little whiskey in her belly. Before I made it into the building, I made a few melon sales from the back of my pickup truck parked out front. The crazy daughter came out to the truck to keep me some company but kept grabbing me in the crotch. Her mother came outside and told me, "When the bitch gets drunk, I can't do a thing with her." Rather than pursue a whiskey transaction that would have been easy to do, I wised up instead and got the hell out of there.

- Two hookers in Richmond City wanted to trade me something, meaning sexual favors, for a melon since they had no cash. I asked them if they were for real. One said she would not do it for one melon, but she would for two!

- Purchasing illegal whiskey as a watermelon salesman was an easy job, so easy that I once made seven purchases out of one house in the city of Alexandria. It was necessary in this area to bring a partner along with me because someone had to stay back and watch the truck. People in this town would steal anything that wasn't nailed down—my produce, my tools, even the truck itself.

- I asked one man on the street if he knew where I could purchase some whiskey. He told me that he did, and so I listened carefully to the directions he was about to give me, or so I thought. It turned out that he had the half-pints lined up inside his coat. That was a sight I had never seen and never saw again except for a similar experience with a man on a bike. He had whiskey in the basket on the front of his bike—curb service, so to speak. Talk about an office on the go!

- It was a hot summer day, and I had had enough—enough of the heat, enough of the sweat, enough of the melons, and enough of the surprisingly slow day for illegal whiskey purchases. After I loaded my truck up, I swung by the home of a dependable whiskey salesman named OG. He was home, so I made two purchases. He peeked out the window of his house in the direction of my truck and asked me how much I wanted for the melons that I had left. I remembered from my recent inventory of the melons that I had eighteen left and was pleasantly surprised when OG purchased them all. When we went to court weeks later, OG still had those watermelons on his mind. He told the judge that he purchased a truckload of melons from me and that it wasn't fair that I had arrested him after that for selling whiskey. I saw him some years later, and he told me he would never forget me or my melons!

- In the town of Crewe, I made purchases from a man who worked at a funeral home. With every purchase, I would give him peaches or melons in return. On the night of the raids, I went to the funeral home. He asked me what I had for him as soon as I walked through the door. I told him to come on out to my truck to see for himself. Instead of watermelons or peaches, I served him two warrants for selling alcoholic beverages while not licensed to do so. He was not a happy man and said that I had played a dirty trick. Oh well!

- I made another buy from a woman. Rather than pay with cash, I traded her in peaches. She told me how much her whiskey was, and I gave her a half basket of peaches. When we went to court, she told the judge that she was not guilty because no money had changed hands. The judge asked her if she thought it was all right to trade peaches for whiskey, and she said, "Yes." He found her guilty because my peaches and her price for whiskey were of equal value.

- I was always worried about parking my truckload of peaches overnight because I did not want them to be stolen or spoiled by the heat and humidity. Rather than park on the street one night, I decided to take my huckster truck to the state police headquarters and park in their secured lot. Wrong decision. The policemen stole more than any group of strangers I ever ran into on the streets. I told myself that they were going to go bad anyway due to the heat and decided not to get too worked up over it.

- For those who wonder from where the produce came, here's the rest of the story. One day, my supervisor called all the investigators up to a farm. When the investigators arrived, they asked what they had been called for and could not believe it when they were told that they were going to pick peaches and watermelons for the day. That's right—we picked the produce ourselves.

One Under the Bed

White Oak Swamp in Westmoreland County is covered with water most of the time. There were quite a number of stills in this area, most of them small with one, two, or three barrels of mash. Violators would dig deep into the ground until they reached a graveled water level to use as a water source. Copper stills with a capacity of forty to fifty gallons were placed accordingly then fired with gas. There was usually a pressure tank pumped up to force gas into the firebox under the still and start the process.

My partner, Mickey Amos, and I raided one still on a very cold day. We would always have a raid plan and decide from which side we would rush the still site. Usually, I would raid from one direction and he would go in from the other. Depending on the situation—time of day, location of the still, number of bootleggers—we might quietly sneak up on the violators or attack abruptly and loudly in order to cause confusion and chaos. I preferred to raid the still like a bat out of hell. It was more fun that way. I would run in screaming and hollering to both scare and surprise the moonshiners, catching all that I could, while the rest would run straight into the arms of my partner on the other side.

Still in Westmoreland County

When raiding a still, most of the time, there would be a number of people there. At the time of this particular raid, there were three violators working. I got very close to the still before they saw me. I jumped up, yelling, and nearly had my hands on all three before two got loose. One ran toward my partner. The other, running in another direction, stopped dead in his tracks when I threatened to shoot. He literally hit the ground. I then commanded him to come back to me, and the dummy did just that. I put the handcuffs on my two while Mickey chased the quick-footed bootlegger into a nearby home and found him under the bed.

Once all three men were captured, we walked to the front of the yard where there was a parked vehicle. I asked if anybody had a key, but no one would fess up. I went over to my car and retrieved an ax out of the back. I then walked back over to the vehicle in question and swung it over my shoulder and into the trunk of the car, leaving a dent. Luckily, my instinct was dead on and there was a case of illegal whiskey locked away. I would have had some explaining to do if not.

Drove into the Still

We raided another still in White Oak Swamp after nearly driving into the site by accident. My partner, Gordon Birkett, and I were driving down a sawmill road after dropping two game officers off to check on some goose hunters. We had some time to kill before we had to drive back and pick them up, so we decided to explore the area a bit and keep our eyes peeled for any unusual activity. We came across a path leading down a steep hill, and I asked my partner to stop the vehicle so that I could get out to investigate. When I positioned myself to peek over the bank, I saw a still in operation down below, with three men working. I whispered back to Birkett to turn off the car before they heard the engine. He asked why, and I told him there was a still in operation as we spoke!

Still in Westmoreland County

We ran down the hill and raided the still in a matter of seconds. I arrested one man and cuffed him to a tree while Birkett arrested another. The third violator took off running through the woods, and I chased after. We ran and ran until we literally could run no longer. There were even times when both of us had to take breaks. The moonshiner would be up ahead, walking off his exhaustion, and I would follow behind him, doing the same. If I got a sudden burst of energy and felt strong enough to chase after him again, he would take off until it was necessary to walk some more. This was a true walking duel. Finally, my commitment to catching the moonshiner won over his to get away. Once he was also placed in cuffs, he asked me how we found them, and I said that we literally drove right in.

Camp 17

In the woods next to Camp 17, which was a convict camp located in Richmond County, I once raided a still with an ATF agent during a thunderstorm. There were several moonshiners in this area, and I had been involved in several raids there before. This was the first time, however, for the ATF agent. He was a big Indian named Bridgewater, and I felt confident that he could hold his own. When we raided the still, there were two violators working. I went in and grabbed one just before he turned and hit me behind the ear. Bridgewater saw this, tackled the violator, and told me to chase down the other since he had this one under control. The shiner I was chasing turned out to be a fourteen-year-old boy who could run like a deer. He led me deep into the woods until I finally caught up to him and managed to place him in handcuffs. Once the chase was over, I could hear a lot of noise coming from the still and decided to cuff the boy to a tree so that I could head back to see what was going on. The boy begged me not to leave him, but I knew it would be too risky to bring him along. When I got back to the still, I saw that the violator had somehow gotten away from Bridgewater. Together, we went back to the tree to retrieve the boy and then on to a place where I knew we would find the other moonshiner.

The one who escaped from Bridgewater served time in the local jail but was considered a trustee and given special privileges. This meant that he was allowed to go home to split wood for his wife. While he was home "splitting wood," she somehow became with child and spent a good portion of her pregnancy with her husband behind bars. I arrested him many times after this and learned that he always put up a good fight.

Still in Richmond County

Drinking Swamp

I located a still on Drinking Swamp Road in Richmond County. I recognized one of the two subjects working the still. His name was PT, he was six-foot-four and could run like hell. My partner and I crawled up very close to the still while the two men were working. I told my partner that the perfect time to raid the still would be when PT headed back to the swamp to get another bucket of water to put into the cooling barrel. I would take PT while he got the other.

Still in Richmond County

This was in the summertime, and the mayflies were worse than ever. The flies are better known as deerflies, but the locals call them mayflies because you don't see them until the month of May. It was all I could do to keep still in the midst of so many mayflies while we waited for the agreed-upon time of attack. When PT finally went toward the swamp again, I was on top of him before he knew what hit him. It was as if he knew I couldn't stand the mayflies any longer. We made the two violators carry the copper still out of the woods just like the flies that nearly carried us away.

When we went to court, the attorney who had PT's case told the judge that he was a sick man. He told the judge to look at how pale he was. Because ole PT was a light-skinned black man, everyone in court got a big laugh out of that one.

The Brass Band

Sometimes moonshiners would have more than one location stored with mash but would use only one still that was moved to and from each site. I located one of these rigs, minus the still, and decided to camp out until the still and the moonshiners arrived. I knew it wouldn't be before long and stayed all night waiting for the violators. The next morning, I was awakened by a noise. It sounded like a brass band coming down the path and heading in my direction. Sure enough, here came two violators carrying a copper still on their backs. The sound I had heard was the branches hitting the copper still along the path. It really did sound like a brass band. I arrested both "band members" for transporting equipment and materials intended for the illegal manufacture of whiskey.

Nervous Bea

My partner and I located a small still in Northumberland County on the edge of the woods near the Lancaster County line. There was a plowed field between the still and a house, where we could see people on the porch. After a little while, I took cover on the other side of the still and waited for the moonshiners to return. Unfortunately, the violator, known to us as Nervous Bea, returned with two dogs that came in and found me. The violator took off running once my presence was known, and I quickly chased after him. The dogs thought we were playing and were running after the both of us, crossing paths along the way. First I would fall over a dog, and then the violator would fall over one. I eventually ran him down in the plowed field, at which point the violator started screaming from the top of his lungs for help. I asked him why he was yelling, and he told me that he got help the last time he was in trouble by doing just that. When I told him that I was a police officer, he felt pretty silly but continued to preach to me the whole car ride into town. He said that God would see to it that he would not get jail time. The next day, I went to check on Nervous and found him to be still in jail.

A Snowy Day on Dragon Run

I received information on a still at the head of Dragon Run in King and Queen County. I followed the lead and had no trouble locating the still. The next day, I went back with my partner to wait for the moonshiners, and it started to snow. Before long, there were about four inches on the ground. Just when the snow started to lighten up, I saw a black man through the flurries walking my way with a dog. Like always, the dog sniffed me out, and the bootlegger went running. I caught him in three steps and placed him under arrest, then handed him over to my partner while I went to check on the contents of the still. The violator must have somehow escaped because I heard my partner yell out to him, ordering him to come back. The man, however, kept on running. We chased him all the way back to a house, his house. He told us that he knew he would be caught and sent to jail but wanted to first see his children before he went away.

Old Man in King George

One of the simplest arrests I ever made was with an ATF agent at a small still in King George County. One of the two violators was an old man who had been very cooperative during the raid. I told him to go over and sit down while we destroyed the still. After we worked up a good sweat axing the equipment into pieces, I asked the old man as we were walking to the state car if he had ever been arrested for making whiskey. He told me that he hadn't. I then asked him if he had ever been arrested for anything else, and he answered, "Yes." I asked him for what, and he told me that he had been arrested for murder! I was in shock and couldn't believe that this old, easygoing man was a murderer. I asked him, "I guess I had better put the cuffs on you then, huh?" It turned out that he had escaped from prison in North Carolina and was now making moonshine in Virginia. You never know!

Daddy's Little Girl

I located a small still in a barn just behind a house. I went up to the house, knocked on the door, and asked the black man who answered if he was the homeowner. I then asked him if he had a key to the barn door because I wanted to take a look inside.

He told me that that wouldn't be necessary because he knew that I knew that there was a still in there. Just as I was arresting the subject and charging him with the violation, one of his two teenage daughters jumped up and fought me all the way to the car. It was obvious that she was daddy's little girl and did not want her daddy to go to jail.

County Official

There was one particularly tricky arrest that took place on a farm where the farmer had helped the moonshiners disguise the route to a still. The disguise was done so well that we would not have located the still if it had not been for a sighting from an airplane patrol. We even drove right up to the gate that was guarding the still the day before but did not see anything suspicious and turned around.

275-gallon still with an upright boiler in King and Queen County

While we were waiting for the supply truck to arrive, we witnessed a not-so-honest county official unlocking the gate on the farm for the moonshiners so they could gain access to the still. Not far behind the gate stood a large still with a capacity of four thousand to six thousand gallons of mash, 2,800 pounds of sugar, and dozens of jars. There were two violators when we raided the still. One was a black male and the other was a young kid wearing a football jersey. My partner grabbed the kid while I cuffed the other. Then we sent the sugar and jars to Camp 17 before destroying the still.

Identical Twins

Some of the biggest stills were in King and Queen County, often with four thousand gallons of mash or more. Most of the still operators came out of Richmond City, Newport News, and Norfolk. My partner, Maxie Broaddus, and I once located a still at an old brick house that we recognized as a still from a previous arrest. It was owned by identical twin brothers from Richmond who were in the produce business. The mash was about to turn sour, and the owners did not want to lose their product, so they came to run the still themselves. These owners didn't normally come in to run their stills, but this was considered an emergency situation. One came in to the still with a farm tractor loaded with coal to fire up the boiler. We let them complete the task at hand before deciding to raid the still, catching two of the three violators immediately. One took off down in the woods, and I gave chase. Because it was dark, I had been chasing him with a flashlight. I finally got the bright idea to cut off the light, at which point the moonshiner ran into a tree, allowing me to cuff him. The next morning, we had breakfast at the violators' expense. They had enough food to feed an army. We cooked eggs, bacon, and coffee. This was a good catch, and we deserved a breakfast for champions.

Finders, Keepers

When we raided stills, there were usually a lot of tools lying around. Once the arrests were finished and the stills destroyed, we would sometimes come back and take these tools for our own personal collection. I had my eye on a nice new pipe wrench that I discovered during a raid. I later saw one of the ATF agents go down in the woods and hide the pipe wrench in the leaves next to a big tree. The next morning, I woke up early and went back to get the item. I left a note written on a sugar bag in its place for my fellow agent. It read, "Not this time." We worked together for a year or more, but he did not say a word nor did I! One day, he couldn't stand it any longer and asked me when I went back to get the wrench. Finders, keepers.

State Record

We still hold the record of the most people caught at a still—twelve (and one got away). It all happened at a large still in King and Queen County that was covered in camouflage. I brought along federal agents to check the mash from this still for a third time, but upon arrival, we found the still to be in full operation with three moonshiners in sight. We raided the still and arrested all three with no problem. Afterward, one of the ATF agents and I walked up a nearby hill overlooking the still and saw a shack covered in tar paper just on the other side. We knew that this shack was housing the still workers, so we walked over to the structure and arrested a man as he was walking out the front door. We went inside and found another in the bed. I yelled for the man to get out of the bed and was surprised when a half-naked woman emerged instead.

At about that time, a vehicle drove up with a carload of people. This had turned out to be a three-ring circus. One of the passengers took off running once the car parked, and I chased after him. He was a big man. We ran and ran until I was able to tackle him. This big man raised his fist as if to fight me until he realized that I was a police officer, not a hijacker. You see, he was like many bootleggers who'd had their whiskey stolen by hijackers one too many times. Hijackers disguised themselves as agents—driving the same black cars as us, wearing the same green uniforms as us, and raiding stills in the same fashion as us. They would run the moonshiners off from their rigs then steal their moonshine, sugar, equipment, and whatever else they could find to use for themselves. Truthfully, bootleggers were more afraid of a hijacker than an ABC agent.

The violator's wrists were so large that I couldn't place handcuffs on him. Because he was genuinely relieved that I wasn't a hijacker, he told me that he wouldn't give me any trouble and gladly followed me back to the still. When we got back, one of the federal officers had the driver from the vehicle in his custody. We sat there talking, trying to catch our breath, when another vehicle with three more subjects pulled up. All three men had been placed in cuffs rather easily when yet another car drove up with even more subjects. We arrested them, waited a bit longer, and decided no one else was coming. Then we placed all the violators in our cars.

Before heading to the jail with what was sure to be a record number of arrests during a single raid, we completed the job by destroying the still with explosives. The explosives got a little out of hand, and we first had to keep the fire in the woods from spreading before we could drive into town and show off our conquests. What a crazy day!

Woody is My Man

There was a well-known moonshining family that lived on Nelson's Millpond and always had a still nearby. They were creative in their operations and used a boat to access their stills across the pond. One brother could run like the wind. The first time I raided one of their stills, I started chasing that brother but was quickly losing ground on him. I began to slow down and took a quick peek back at the still behind me to find that the other brother had not run. I turned back to arrest him and asked, "What's your name, son?" "Woody," he replied. "Woody, why didn't you run?" I asked. He responded, "Because I only have one leg." I was speechless. Every time after that, when we raided one of the their stills, I would jokingly say, "I'll take Woody!"

There were three people at the still, but the third claimed that he had nothing to do with the operation. We arrested him anyway because we witnessed otherwise; I saw him sawing wood. When these violators were taken to court, this particular man told the judge that he was only at the house doing some painting and was innocent. He got time in jail with the two brothers because I had informed the judge of what actually happened. It didn't matter how much or how little you participated in the moonshining business. If you were involved, you were guilty.

Moonshiner Disguise

We came across a very large still in the middle of a swamp on the edge of Essex County near the Caroline County line. We could tell from afar that the still was in operation because we could hear the moonshiners talking. There were two trucks parked, one with a load of jars, the other with slabs that were used to fire the still. My partner and I saw one of the two moonshiners coming up the swamp with a case of illegal whiskey on his shoulder. He was knee-high in water. I told my partner, "You take him, and I will go get the other." My partner took off after the violator who dropped the forty-five-pound case of moonshine and started to run in the opposite direction. Without skipping a beat, I cleverly picked up two of the cases of jars, placing one under my arm and the other on my shoulder, much like a moonshiner going into the still would. I walked through the water and right up to the other shiner, who was pouring moonshine into a jar. He thought that I was his friend coming back and never ran; he never even looked up. That was an easy arrest. This still had eight boxes of mash, each four hundred gallons. The owner of this still had told the two boys that he left to run it, "If this still is raided you had better run, and run fast, because if Bobby Watkins catches you, he will beat the crap out of you." I don't know where he got that information from—ha!

Someone Spiked the Iced Tea

After receiving information on a still in Essex County near Indian Neck, I had a state trooper drop me out to survey the area, and I asked him to pick me up a little later on. It was easy to locate the still, and even easier to raid it and catch the two still workers. The trooper returned to pick me up, along with the two moonshiners, a few hours later. Before we left the still site, one of the violators asked if he could grab the jar of iced tea that was sitting on one of the mash barrels because he was thirsty. The trooper agreed and on we went, me in the front passenger seat and the two of them in the back.

On the way to the jail, the trooper ran into a car accident. I told the violators to stay in the car while I jumped out to help the trooper work the wreck. When I got back to the car, the two violators were drunk as hell. It turned out that the iced tea was actually moonshine with a little coloring in it. What did they care? They were going to jail anyway.

This particular still contained its mash in steel barrels rather than wood, which was dangerous because the steel rusted easily and usually carried insecticide or other harmful products in a previous life. I told the violators that I should shoot them for making bad moonshine. One of the men said that he had tested it by placing a penny in the jar and knew that the moonshine was fine because it didn't turn the penny brown. Because that was no accurate test of the quality of the whiskey, I had only gotten madder and told him that he would be a lucky man if he got away without me shooting him.

Barn Party

I had a call from a game warden who told me that he had run into a bunch of black string strung in the woods. I knew of a moonshiner whose mode of operation (MO) was to mark the perimeter of his rig with string so that if it were broken he would know someone had been there. I followed the directions from the warden and found the still located in an old barn. The whole barn was filled up with distilling equipment, eight thousand gallons of mash, an upright boiler, and cases of moonshine. The barn was wrapped in black paper on the inside so that you could not see the lights from outside or what was going on inside. The smokestack to the boiler was shoved in a hole, and a basketball goal was used to cover the hole when the still wasn't in use. This was a clever disguise that I hadn't seen before.

Confiscated moonshine found in King and Queen County

We stayed in the woods for two days, watching the still site and waiting for a moonshiner to step foot on the premises. Because the stakeout had taken longer than anticipated, I called and asked the sheriff to contact my wife to let her know that I would be out for a few days. He agreed but forgot to actually do so. She had some not-so-kind words for the sheriff later!

Finally, at the edge of dark one evening, the violators came in with fuel and supplies. We raided the still only a few minutes after their arrival. One of the men ran into a weed field, and I followed, finding him laying on his back a few steps later. He told me that he had heart trouble and needed his medicine.

This violator went by the name HW and was one of the big-time moonshiners in the area who was also very well liked. When we went to court, the case was dismissed on a technicality. In the search warrant, I described the house that the violators were living in as a story-and-a-half building when actually it was a two-story house. The lawyer convinced the jury that it was the wrong house, so HW got off scot-free. One of the members of the jury was seen talking to HW the day before. HW's charges were dropped very suspiciously, if you ask me.

Fox and Hounds

It was a beautiful fall day in the upper end of King and Queen County. My partner, Gordon Birkett, and I had located a nice still a few days before. We returned to wait for the moonshiners to come in and start their run. We were lying on a hillside in the warm sunshine, listening to a pack of hounds running a fox. All at once, here comes the fox right by us. My partner said to me, "Watch this!" If you've ever heard someone say that before, you know that what's about to happen will likely be memorable— either as one of the most amazing sights you've ever seen or one of the most foolish moments you've witnessed on someone else's behalf. And so, Birkett went to the crest of the hill, laid down, and waited for the dogs. The whole pack of hounds, close to twenty, came over the hill with their noses to the ground in hot pursuit of the fox, not paying attention to anything else. My partner jumped up, making a loud growling sound and waving his arms. Well, if you could have seen those dogs—of all the yelping and falling over each other that you have ever seen. We had a good laugh between us that day. I still get a little chuckle when I think about him. Sometimes the predator becomes the prey.

Pepsi-Cola Caper

I located a nice still in Essex County between Lloyds and Eleven. We returned Saturday morning because we expected the still to be running by that time, but it was still not operating. We brought six Pepsi cans with us and put them down the hill in the cold water so that they would be ready to drink the next day. When we came back, the still was in operation, and my partner and I were able to catch the violators in little to no time. It was a hot day, and my partner expressed his desire to the moonshiners for a cold drink. He specifically mentioned that a Pepsi sure would taste good. After a decent amount of chatter, I said to him, "Well, why don't you go to the swamp and get one?" When he came up the hill with two cold Pepsi-Colas, the moonshiners sat in disbelief with their mouths wide open. They couldn't believe that we had been watching them for days. One of the violators told me that the reason they decided to run the still on a Sunday was because they thought I would be in church. I told him that that is what I thought they would be thinking.

Drunk Coon

A hunter from Westmoreland County once told me that he had been coon hunting and that the coon he found was acting crazy and would not go up the tree. He gave the coon to an old man who was going to eat it. In cleaning the coon, the man found the coon's stomach to be full of mash. In other words, the coon was drunk when the hunter came across him and literally could not figure out how to go up the tree. I again spoke with the hunter and found out exactly where he found the coon. We walked the area described by the hunter until we eventually found a still that was mashed in and ready to run. We went in to check the still several times until it finally went into operation. The culprits were a seventy-eight-year-old grandfather and his fourteen-year-old grandson. The old man was teaching his youngest grandson how to master the art of making moonshine, and he was making good stuff, too. He did something unusual that I had never seen done before. He left the grain in the bag and put the whole bag in the water with the sugar and yeast. It was a smart move because it saved him a step. The men then didn't have to strain the mash before putting it into the still. After I caught them both, I went to the nearest house and asked the man that lived there if I could use his phone to report my findings. He turned out to be a preacher who lived there and said that it was the devil making moonshine on a Sunday morning.

Birthday Suit

It can be funny how you establish a relationship with an informant. I raided a still one time and arrested three men. Two of the three violators told me that the third wasn't involved in making the moonshine. They said he was only there for a quick drink. The man said that this was true and that his family was waiting back at the house for him so they could go to a birthday party. I thought that his story might be legitimate only because of the way he was dressed. He was wearing a blue suit with a red tie. I took this man up to his house for verification and found his wife and young children, dressed in their Sunday best, waiting for him in the parlor. Turns out his story was true. Because I had already arrested the man, it was required that he appear in court to defend himself. When the court date arrived, I went to bat for him and the judge sided in his favor as well. He turned out to be a good informant.

School Bus Story

My partner and I located a still in the upper end of King and Queen County near Newtown that was mashed in and ready to run. In a very short time, two moonshiners came in and got to work. We let them get the fire started, the first step in the process of making whiskey, before we raided the site and arrested both men. After talking with them and filing our necessary reports, my ears perked up when I heard one say that a school bus would be there soon with more workers. I asked him what was he talking about. "What school bus?" He continued to explain that one of the still operators also worked as a school bus driver and would be headed this way once he dropped the children off from school. After putting him and his counterpart in handcuffs, we told them to act like they were working so that we could successfully set up the third shiner.

I even helped them fill the still up with mash so that it would keep running. I remember seeing a mouse in the mash when I tried to pour it into the still through a funnel. The mash would not run through the funnel because of the dead animal. Because most of the stills I raided were dirty, this really was no surprise.

As promised by the moonshiners, two more men drove up to the still in a school bus soon after. We arrested them also, and transported all four to the closest county jail since there wasn't one in King and Queen at the time. I talked to the violators on the way and got information on another still in the same area. The men I arrested usually wanted to know who turned them in, so I was always careful with whom I shared information. If you worked things right, you could get information from anyone about a competitor's still.

Icehouse

Finding a still that was ready to run was like hitting the jackpot. I once found one next to a millpond. It was placed near an old icehouse that people used back in the old days to store cut ice from the pond for the summer. I hid in a hole inside the icehouse where I could look down at the still. After a short while, I saw a man, woman, and child approaching the still site, all carrying sugar and jars. They also had two dogs with them. I knew the dogs were going to find me so I quickly mapped out my attack plan. Just as I expected, the dogs came up, looked down in the icehouse hole, and started to bark. I sat waiting until the violator came over to see what had gotten the dogs stirred up. When he looked over the boards, I jumped out of the hole like a jack-in-the-box. Once I got a good handle on the moonshiner, I yelled for the woman and child to go back to the house. She must have misunderstood what I said and asked her husband to please repeat my orders. The violator told her to get her ass back to the house, "Now!" Once the arrest was finished at the still site, I took him back to the house to bid farewell for now to his wife and nine children. Over time, he turned out to be one of my best informants.

Almost Chauffeur

I arrested an old bootlegger at a small still in the upper end of Essex County. It was a forty-gallon copper still with two fifty-gallon barrels of mash. After destroying the still and other equipment, I took him to the magistrate, which we did in the old days. Since the magistrate knew the violator, he gave him bond and set his case to be tried at a later date in court.

By this time, it was about four o'clock in the morning. The

violator and I had become friends, being that I had arrested him many times, so he asked me if I would give him a ride home. I didn't mind and told him I would. Well, we were driving along chatting about the times that I had caught him and the times that he had gotten away. Yawning, I told my friend how sleepy and tired I was. He kindly asked me, "You want me to drive, Mr. Watkins?" I wasn't sleepy enough to have a bootlegger driving my state car! This was my last still arrest before retirement.

Conclusion

As I reflect on my days in uniform, I find myself laughing out loud, scratching my head, having sweaty palms, and sometimes sitting in disbelief. There's one thing I'm sure of: I never met a bootlegger I didn't like. I've shared these stories with family and friends but have dreamed for so long of putting pen to paper. After being interviewed by a few newspapers, giving presentations in the community, meeting celebrity moonshiners, and having my very own professional photo shoot, I finally decided it was time to do just that. I dedicated so much of my life to chasing moonshiners and have found much pleasure in recounting these stories. I hope you, too, have enjoyed this glimpse into my past, and believe me when I say that *almost* every word is true!

Bobby Watkins and ATF agent taking inventory after a raid

Glossary

ABC (noun): Alcoholic Beverage Control, the public state agency with law enforcement responsibilities concerning the manufacture, transportation, and distribution of alcoholic beverages; state equivalent to the federal ATF

ATF (noun): Bureau of Alcohol, Tobacco, and Firearms, the federal agency with law enforcement responsibilities for matters including the manufacture, transportation, and distribution of alcoholic beverages, tobacco, and firearms; federal equivalent to the state ABC; now called the Bureau of Alcohol, Tobacco, Firearms, and Explosives

boiler (noun): container that serves as the heart of a still and heats the mash until it becomes vapor; commonly made from stainless steel pots, copper barrels, and beer kegs

bootleg (noun): illegal whiskey; (verb): to illegally manufacture, sell, or transport for sale alcohol; also called hooch, devil's brew, white mule, rotgut, moonshine, IW, white lightning

doubler (noun): see "thumper"

fermentation (noun): breakdown of sugar into an acid or alcohol; chemical decomposition of an organic substance in the absence of oxygen

huckster (noun): a person who drives and sells from a produce truck lay worm (noun): straight sections of copper that are connected by elbow turns and laid into a body of water then used to cool the alcohol; lay worms are only found with large stills

lye (noun): a chemical used in cleaning products; a common poisonous ingredient used in the distillation process of alcohol to hasten fermentation

mash (noun): a combination of grain, sugar, and water used in the fermentation process; if the mash has gone sour, it is no longer good

moonshine (noun): see "bootleg"

nip joint (noun): an unlicensed establishment where liquor is usually sold by the shot

rig (noun): the components that make up a still, including the boiler, the worm, the thumper, etc.

thumper (noun): a second container sometimes used in the distillation process that is not directly heated and whose primary function is to collect the mash overflow that hasn't yet turned into vapor and helps to prevent the moonshine from becoming cloudy; also known as "doubler"

worm (noun): coiled tubing in a container of water used to cool the alcohol; usually made from copper

Appendix

Various Virginia ABC Data Reports,
Informant Letters and Maps

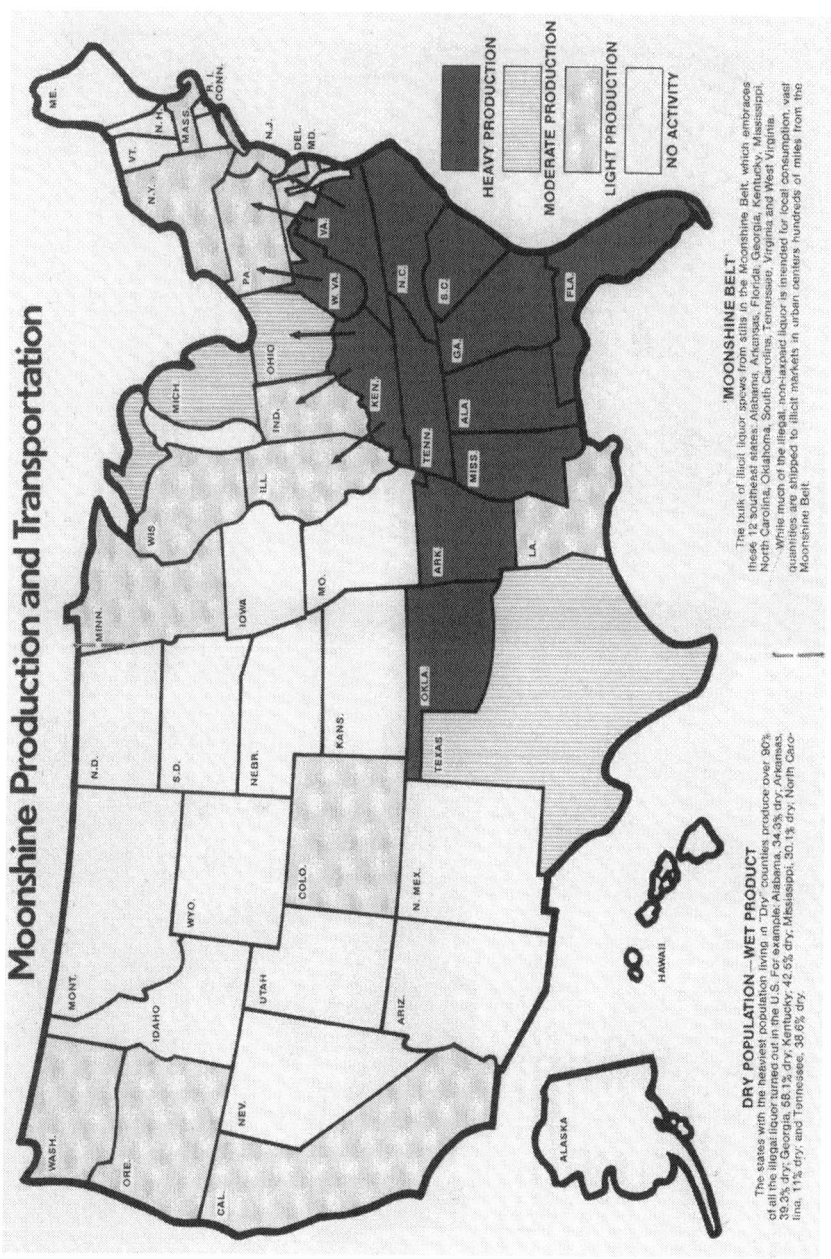

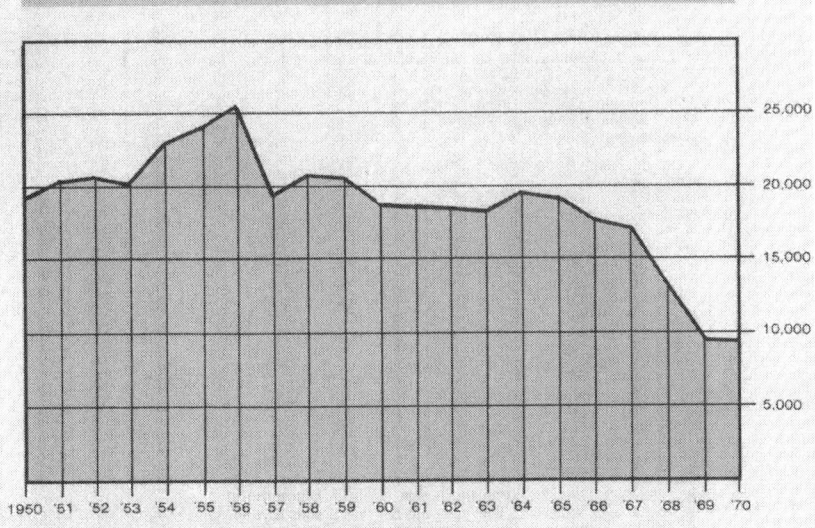

STILL SEIZURES 1950-70

	SEIZURES BY FEDERAL AGENTS	SEIZURES BY STATE-LOCAL AGENTS	TOTAL REPORTED STILL SEIZURES
1950	10,206	9,614	19,820
1951	10,250	10,225	20,475
1952	10,685	9,909	20,594
1953	10,530	9,479	20,009
1954	11,943	10,995	22,938
1955	13,717	9,997	23,714
1956	14,003	11,605	25,608
1957	9,978	9,703	19,681
1958	9,185	11,470	20,655
1959	9,519	10,897	20,416
1960	6,593	12,208	18,801
1961	7,175	11,418	18,593
1962	6,295	12,356	18,651
1963	6,562	11,898	18,460
1964	7,377	12,581	19,958
1965	7,654	11,737	19,391
1966	6,946	10,828	17,774
1967	6,437	10,646	17,083
1968	4,995	8,070	13,065
1969	4,139	5,508	9,647
1970	5,088	4,434	9,522

Courtesy of Licensed Beverage Industries, Inc. *"Moonshine: The Poison Business"*

STILL SEIZURES 1970

STATE	TOTAL STATE AND LOCAL	FEDERAL	TOTAL FEDERAL, STATE AND LOCAL
ALABAMA	1,529	1,259	2,788
ARKANSAS	9	31	40
CALIFORNIA	3	2	5
COLORADO	2	3	5
DELAWARE	0	1	1
FLORIDA	31	116	147
GEORGIA	1,618	1,224	2,842
ILLINOIS	0	6	6
INDIANA	3	3	6
KENTUCKY	10	73	83
LOUISIANA	2	4	6
MARYLAND	6	5	11
MASSACHUSETTS	0	3	3
MICHIGAN	0	14	14
MINNESOTA	0	1	1
MISSISSIPPI	183	334	517
NEW JERSEY	7	3	10
NEW YORK	0	2	2
NORTH CAROLINA	419	874	1,293
OHIO	5	25	30
OKLAHOMA	3	36	39
OREGON	3	0	3
PENNSYLVANIA	7	3	10
SOUTH CAROLINA	180	429	609
TENNESSEE	139	426	565
TEXAS	8	4	12
VIRGINIA	258	175	433
WASHINGTON	2	0	2
WEST VIRGINIA	6	32	38
WISCONSIN	1	0	1
TOTAL	4,434	5,088	9,522

Courtesy of Licensed Beverage Industries, Inc. *"Moonshine: The Poison Business"*

ANNUAL REPORT OF ACTIVITIES

1961-1962

NAME	TERRITORY	RAIDS	ARRESTS	STILLS	BUYS	VEHICLES
H. P. Mapp	Accomac	98	16	31	1	2
	Northampton	18	3	8	0	2
		116	19	39	1	4
G. E. Schucker	Norfolk City	224	96	0	19	3
S. G. Howell	Portsmouth City	249	325	0	3	7
P. L. Shaw	South Norfolk City	117	42	0	0	2
W. G. Johnson	Suffolk City	27	12	0	0	1
	Virginia Beach City	1	0	0	0	0
	Nansemond	55	52	21	1	11
	Norfolk	75	34	12	2	7
	Princess Anne	11	11	6	0	0
		759	572	39	25	31
G. T. Dixon	Hampton City	42	28	1	11	2
P. L. Powers	Newport News City	407	199	6	14	13
W. A. Caton	Williamsburg City	0	0	0	0	0
	Gloucester	3	3	1	2	0
	Isle of Wight	73	52	17	4	3
	James City	30	27	20	0	2
	Mathews	0	0	0	0	0
	York	19	28	4	2	5
		574	337	49	33	25
F. W. Enroughty	Fredericksburg City	6	2	0	1	0
G. P. Smethie	Richmond City	863	860	2	49	27
R. L. Stringer	Caroline	13	2	6	0	0
G. P. Hambleton	Charles City	47	32	45	0	4
H. K. Nelson	Chesterfield	20	10	7	1	1
B. G. Bourne	Goochland	31	17	27	0	8
	Hanover	38	26	15	2	3
	Henrico	12	7	4	0	3
	King William	2	3	2	0	0
	New Kent	9	1	7	0	1
	Spotsylvania	1	0	1	0	0
		1042	960	116	53	47
M. G. Broaddus	Essex	32	17	9	3	0
R. F. Watkins	King George	2	0	1	0	0
	King & Queen	11	10	3	0	1
	Lancaster	0	0	0	0	0
	Middlesex	3	5	0	2	1
	Northumberland	1	1	0	0	0
	Richmond	10	6	6	0	1
	Westmoreland	16	11	8	1	1
		75	50	27	6	4

1961-1962

NAME	TERRITORY	RAIDS	ARRESTS	STILLS	BUYS	VEHICLES
E. L. Hubbard	Charlottesville City	12	9	0	11	0
M. H. Birckhead	Albemarle	21	21	2	12	0
	Culpeper	3	0	2	0	0
	Fluvanna	9	5	3	0	1
	Greene	14	3	5	0	0
	Louisa	24	11	9	1	6
	Madison	5	2	3	0	0
	Orange	6	1	1	0	0
		94	52	25	24	7
L. W. Carroll	Harrisonburg City	0	3	0	2	0
	Staunton City	3	8	0	1	0
	Waynesboro City	0	0	0	0	0
	Augusta	0	0	0	0	0
	Highland	0	0	0	0	0
	Page	7	8	3	2	6
	Rockingham	5	7	1	2	0
		15	26	4	7	6
G. M. Whiteside	Buena Vista City	1	6	0	2	0
	Clifton Forge City	2	4	0	1	0
	Covington City	18	9	0	7	1
	Alleghany	30	3	2	2	1
	Bath	14	0	0	0	0
	Botetourt	19	7	1	1	1
	Rockbridge	6	1	0	0	0
		90	30	3	13	3
H. C. Matthews	Lynchburg City	46	11	0	0	0
R. L. Hayes	Amherst	62	4	4	1	0
	Appomattox	30	18	1	17	0
	Bedford	42	7	2	2	1
	Buckingham	9	15	1	13	1
	Campbell	32	5	1	3	0
	Nelson	64	8	9	0	5
		285	68	18	36	7
E. M. Lewis	Danville City	301	103	0	1	8
R. C. Larson	South Boston City	48	11	0	0	2
G. A. Jones	Halifax	79	31	8	0	4
	Pittsylvania	202	81	20	0	2
		630	226	28	1	16

1961-1962

NAME	TERRITORY	RAIDS	ARRESTS	STILLS	BUYS	VEHICLES
G. A. Martin	Radford City	5	3	0	3	0
M. W. Prillaman	Roanoke City	114	92	0	34	18
J. A. Powell	Craig	7	14	2	8	0
J. R. DuBose	Floyd	47	23	16	0	1
	Giles	18	7	7	8	0
	Montgomery	17	3	3	0	0
	Roanoke	65	31	4	6	4
		273	173	32	59	23
J. A. Hix	Franklin	206	130	92	10	29
J. A. Bowman						
V. K. Stoneman						
C. D. Godsey	Martinsville City	56	24	0	3	6
S. A. Conner	Henry	123	88	29	6	9
S. L. Simmons	Patrick	143	78	48	1	7
		322	190	77	10	22
R. P. Richardson	Galax City	13	8	0	0	0
W. W. Moore	Bland	1	0	0	0	0
	Carroll	80	19	7	5	3
	Grayson	69	20	10	10	0
	Pulaski	11	1	0	0	0
	Smyth	21	12	6	12	1
	Tazewell	45	20	4	4	4
	Wythe	15	13	0	9	3
		255	93	27	40	11
E. G. Younce	Buchanan	69	43	25	20	2
	Dickenson	83	40	27	3	1
	Russell	5	5	1	2	0
		157	88	53	25	3
D. J. Davidson	Bristol City	15	14	0	1	0
W. E. Salley	Norton City	38	15	0	3	1
	Lee	36	15	8	2	0
	Scott	11	9	6	0	0
	Washington	15	15	4	16	0
	Wise	73	39	30	5	0
		188	107	48	27	1

TOTALS

SUPERVISOR	DISTRICT	RAIDS	ARRESTS	STILLS	BUYS	VEHICLES
F. D. Tymosko	Eastern	3,442	2,351	372	165	183
V. O. Smith	Central	1,393	525	122	100	55
A. L. Fulcher	Western	1,401	781	329	171	89
		6,236	3,657	823	436	327

VIRGINIA ALCOHOLIC BEVERAGE CONTROL BOARD

DIVISION OF ENFORCEMENT

REPORT OF ACTIVITIES FOR FISCAL YEAR 1961-1962

Number of investigations conducted	28,157
Number of raids conducted	6,236
Number of purchases from known violators	436
Number of arrests	3,657
Number of convictions	3,396
Number of dismissals	164
Number of cases nolle prossed	314
Number of interdictions	144
Total fines imposed in State and Federal Courts	$233,086.00
Total fines suspended	$4,485.00
Total months jail sentences imposed	9,433
Total months jail sentences to serve	3,343
Total months jail sentences suspended	6,090
Number of defendants put under peace bonds	179
Amount of Bonds imposed	$53,000.00
Amount of Bonds forfeited	$3,000.00
Number of gallons of whiskey seized and destroyed	22,734
Number of gallons of mash seized and destroyed	379,589
Number of stills seized and destroyed	823
Number of vehicles seized	327
Number of pounds of sugar seized	60,420
Number of days worked	13,090
Number of hours worked	128,753
Number of miles traveled	1,007,792

The approximate value of the seizures listed above is as follows:

60,692.9 gallons whiskey at $12.00 per gallon (Mash seized and destroyed at stills condensed to whiskey at a ratio of 10:1)	$728,314.80
823 stills at various prices	146,350.00
327 vehicles at various prices	136,175.00
1 boat & motor	250.00
60,420 pounds sugar at $8.50 per hundred	5,135.70
Miscellaneous articles and equipment	14,789.40
Total	$1,031,014.90
Amount of fines imposed	$233,086.00
Amount of bonds forfeited	3,000.00
Grand Total	$1,267,100.90

VIRGINIA ALCOHOLIC BEVERAGE CONTROL BOARD

DIVISION OF ENFORCEMENT

MONTHLY REPORT OF ACTIVITIES FOR SEPTEMBER, 1962

I. Results of cases disposed of in September

Number of convictions	300
Number of dismissals	24
Number of cases not prosecuted	35
Number of interdictions	1
Amount of fines imposed	$18,445.00
Amount of fines suspended	$85.00
Total months jail sentences imposed	1,026
Total months jail sentences to serve	632
Total months jail sentences suspended	394
Number of defendants put under Bond	11
Amount of Bonds imposed	$ 3,500.00
Amount of Bonds forfeited	$400.00

II. Stills, equipment, etc., seized during September

Item	Price	Total Value
67 stills	Various prices	$ 20,465.00
25 automobiles	Various prices	16,100.00
3 trucks	Various prices	1,250.00
2,700 pounds sugar	$8.50 per hundred	229.50
1,900 pounds coke	$1.50 per hundred	28.50
301 cases of jars	$ .90 per case	270.90
Miscellaneous articles and equipment		544.30
2,240 gallons whiskey and 30,950 gallons mash reduced to whiskey at a ratio of 10:1, valued at $12.00 per gallon		$ 64,020.00
Total		$102,908.20
Amount of fines imposed		18,445.00
Amount of Bonds forfeited		400.00
Total		$121,753.20

III. Activities of Investigators

Number of investigations	2,162
Number of raids conducted	490
Number of arrests	284
Number of days worked	1,068
Number of hours worked	11,075
Number of miles traveled	84,864
Number of counties worked in	92
Number of cities worked in	24

ANNUAL REPORT OF ACTIVITIES

1962-1963

NAME	TERRITORY	RAIDS	ARRESTS	STILLS	BUYS	VEHICLES
H. P. Mapp	Accomac	69	12	22	1	1
	Northampton	63	13	10	0	0
		132	25	32	1	1
G. E. Schucker	Chesapeake City	213	256	6	74	16
S. G. Howell	Norfolk City	259	202	0	51	3
P. L. Shaw	Portsmouth City	244	323	0	65	4
W. G. Johnson	Suffolk City	10	8	0	0	0
	Virginia Beach City	18	16	7	0	7
	Nansemond	35	43	16	0	4
		779	848	29	190	34
G. T. Dixon	Hampton City	36	24	2	13	2
P. L. Powers	Newport News City	469	239	3	59	10
W. A. Caton	Williamsburg City	0	0	0	0	0
	Gloucester	1	0	1	0	0
	Isle of Wight	38	19	17	0	7
	James City	24	20	20	0	3
	Mathews	1	2	1	0	0
	York	12	13	8	0	3
		581	317	52	72	25
F. W. Enroughty	Fredericksburg City	0	0	0	0	0
G. P. Smethie	Richmond City	823	752	2	28	34
R. L. Stringer	Caroline	18	7	9	0	2
G. P. Hambleton	Charles City	41	25	42	0	5
H. K. Nelson	Chesterfield	13	6	8	0	0
B. G. Bourne	Goochland	42	18	19	1	2
	Hanover	32	15	11	1	4
	Henrico	17	19	5	4	4
	King William	6	9	5	0	6
	New Kent	7	7	7	0	5
	Spotsylvania	0	0	0	0	0
		999	858	108	34	62
R. F. Watkins	Essex	31	16	13	0	1
	King George	10	7	2	1	1
	King & Queen	12	14	5	0	6
	Lancaster	4	1	3	0	0
	Middlesex	0	0	0	0	0
	Northumberland	0	0	0	0	0
	Richmond	12	6	6	0	0
	Westmoreland	3	5	3	0	3
		72	49	32	1	11

1962-1963

NAME	TERRITORY	RAIDS	ARRESTS	STILLS	BUYS	VEHICLES
H. McMillion	Amelia	25	15	4	0	4
J. W. Newsome, Jr.	Cumberland	8	7	4	0	2
	Nottoway	15	16	0	0	2
	Powhatan	23	16	10	2	3
	Prince Edward	1	1	0	0	0
		72	55	18	2	11
T. J. Leftwich	Colonial Heights City	5	4	0	0	2
C. E. Costley	Hopewell City	15	5	0	3	1
	Petersburg City	472	96	0	3	7
	Dinwiddie	36	17	6	0	3
	Prince George	20	10	6	0	5
	Surry	16	5	10	0	3
		564	137	22	6	21
T. B. Turner	Franklin City	5	5	0	6	0
A. W. Chappell, Jr.	Greensville	34	24	7	0	1
	Southampton	134	68	60	24	1
	Sussex	25	13	6	0	3
		198	110	73	30	5
M. K. Bryant	Alexandria City	65	31	0	3	1
	Fairfax City	0	0	0	0	0
	Falls Church City	2	0	0	0	0
	Arlington	13	2	0	1	0
	Fairfax	37	25	1	10	2
	Fauquier	13	8	3	1	0
	Prince William	29	19	2	9	3
	Stafford	5	1	1	1	0
		164	86	7	25	6
H. H. Creedle	Brunswick	42	8	9	1	0
B. P. Epperson	Charlotte	25	11	6	2	2
	Lunenburg	48	25	6	0	0
	Mecklenburg	69	29	12	1	2
		184	74	33	4	4
H. C. Pangle	Winchester City	18	7	0	2	1
	Clarke	11	2	1	2	0
	Frederick	7	0	1	0	0
	Loudoun	7	0	0	0	0
	Rappahannock	20	3	6	1	0
	Shenandoah	35	16	2	10	0
	Warren	10	1	2	1	0
		108	29	12	16	1

1962-1963

NAME	TERRITORY	RAIDS	ARRESTS	STILLS	BUYS	VEHICLES
E. L. Hubbard	Charlottesville	6	6	0	3	0
M. H. Birckhead	Albemarle	15	11	7	1	0
	Culpeper	3	0	1	0	0
	Fluvanna	7	2	0	1	0
	Greene	17	9	6	0	0
	Louisa	18	7	12	0	4
	Madison	6	0	4	0	0
	Orange	0	0	0	0	0
		72	35	30	5	4
J. C. Wilfong	Harrisonburg City	7	0	0	0	0
	Staunton City	15	30	0	25	0
	Waynesboro City	9	8	0	7	1
	Augusta	2	5	0	5	0
	Highland	1	0	1	0	0
	Page	5	7	1	1	0
	Rockingham	16	8	1	5	0
		55	58	3	43	1
G. M. Whiteside	Buena Vista City	8	17	0	14	0
	Clifton Forge City	5	3	0	3	0
	Covington City	12	6	0	6	0
	Alleghany	22	2	1	1	0
	Bath	3	0	0	0	0
	Botetourt	32	8	8	3	0
	Rockbridge	2	2	0	3	0
		84	38	9	30	0
H. C. Matthews	Lynchburg City	33	24	0	8	4
R. L. Hayes	Amherst	33	1	3	0	1
	Appomattox	5	1	0	0	1
	Bedford	37	34	13	3	7
	Buckingham	11	3	0	1	1
	Campbell	31	9	3	0	3
	Nelson	31	8	1	0	1
		181	80	20	12	18
E. M. Lewis	Danville City	274	115	0	6	14
R. C. Larson	South Boston City	56	18	0	2	3
G. A. Jones	Halifax	92	55	21	3	12
	Pittsylvania	151	87	15	4	11
		573	275	36	15	40

1962-1963

NAME	TERRITORY	RAIDS	ARRESTS	STILLS	BUYS	VEHICLES
G. A. Martin	Radford City	4	1	0	0	0
J. A. Powell	Roanoke City	318	114	0	5	19
J. R. DuBose	Craig	6	4	3	0	2
	Floyd	26	8	6	0	2
	Giles	26	14	8	5	1
	Montgomery	32	30	3	28	0
	Roanoke	73	45	1	5	3
		485	216	21	43	27
J. A. Bowman	Franklin	168	88	68	6	10
J. A. Hix						
V. K. Stoneman						
C. D. Godsey	Martinsville City	41	13	0	0	0
S. A. Conner	Henry	96	81	17	14	11
S. L. Simmons	Patrick	143	76	41	6	5
		280	170	58	20	16
R. P. Richardson	Galax City	8	7	0	4	1
W. W. Moore	Bland	3	1	0	1	0
	Carroll	73	17	10	0	0
	Grayson	52	16	3	0	1
	Pulaski	31	19	1	6	1
	Smyth	10	5	3	1	1
	Tazewell	28	9	4	0	3
	Wythe	17	12	0	6	1
		222	86	21	18	8
E. G. Younce	Buchanan	80	39	25	15	4
A. C. Farmer, Jr.	Dickenson	96	74	27	13	2
	Russell	14	12	2	3	2
		190	125	54	31	8
D. J. Davidson	Bristol City	32	78	0	73	0
W. E. Salley	Norton City	14	5	0	0	0
	Lee	20	10	6	0	0
	Scott	28	15	8	6	4
	Washington	8	15	3	5	1
	Wise	55	39	24	13	1
		157	162	41	97	6

*** ***

TOTALS

SUPERVISOR	DISTRICT	RAIDS	ARRESTS	STILLS	BUYS	VEHICLES
F. D. Tymosko	Eastern	3,561	2,485	373	361	176
J. L. Blackburn	Central	1,257	589	143	125	68
A. L. Fulcher	Western	1,502	847	263	215	75
		6,320	3,921	779	701	319

VIRGINIA ALCOHOLIC BEVERAGE CONTROL BOARD

DIVISION OF ENFORCEMENT

MONTHLY REPORT OF ACTIVITIES FOR MARCH, 1964

I. Results of cases disposed of in March

Number of convictions	212
Number of dismissals	11
Number of cases not prosecuted	14
Number of interdictions	31
Amount of fines imposed	$ 13,845.00
Amount of fines suspended	0
Total months jail sentences imposed	749
Total months jail sentences to serve	418
Total months jail sentences suspended	331
Number of defendants put under Bond	7
Amount of Bonds imposed	$ 8,200.00

II. Stills, equipment, etc., seized during March

Item	Price	Total Value
75 stills	Various prices	$ 10,070.00
25 automobiles	Various prices	7,550.00
1 truck		250.00
1,110 pounds sugar	$8.50 per hundred	94.35
1,450 pounds meal	$4.50 per hundred	65.25
153 cases of jars	$2.00 per case	306.00
Miscellaneous articles and equipment		755.15

1,415 gallons whiskey and 28,710 gallons mash reduced to whiskey at a ratio of 10:1, valued at $12.00 per gallon	$ 51,432.00
Total	$ 70,216.75
Amount of fines imposed	13,845.00
Amount of Bonds forfeited	0
Total	$ 84,061.75

III. Activities of Investigators

Number of investigations	2,684
Number of raids conducted	503
Number of arrests	295
Number of days worked	1,208
Number of hours worked	11,900
Number of miles traveled	97,492
Number of counties worked in	90
Number of cities worked in	23

VIRGINIA ALCOHOLIC BEVERAGE CONTROL BOARD

DIVISION OF ENFORCEMENT

REPORT OF ACTIVITIES FOR FISCAL YEAR 1965-1966

Number of investigations conducted	28,587
Number of raids conducted	4,428
Number of purchases from known violators	753
Number of arrests	3,346
Number of convictions	3,282
Number of dismissals	235
Number of cases nolle prossed	180
Number of interdictions	103
Total fines imposed in State and Federal Court	$ 237,430.00
Total fines suspended	11,755.00
Total months jail sentences imposed	8,215
Total months jail sentences to serve	2,824
Total months jail sentences suspended	5,391
Number of defendants put under peace bonds	46
Amount of Bonds imposed	$ 26,550.00
Amount of Bonds forfeited	600.00
Number of gallons of whiskey seized	15,341
Number of gallons of mash seized and destroyed	141,415
Number of stills seized and destroyed	558
Number of vehicles seized	210
Number of pounds of sugar seized	24,858
Number of days worked	17,787
Number of hours worked	129,676
Number of miles traveled	1,067,385

The approximate value of the seizures listed above is as follows:

29,682.5 gallons whiskey at $12.00 per gallon	$ 356,190.00
(Mash seized and destroyed at stills condensed to whiskey at a ratio of 10:1)	
558 stills at various prices	111,366.00
210 vehicles at various prices	71,860.00
1 farm tractor	100.00
1 u-haul trailer	150.00
2 jeeps	450.00
24,858 pounds sugar at $10.50 per hundred	2,610.09
Miscellaneous articles and equipment	7,596.61
Total	$ 550,322.70
Amount of fines imposed	$ 237,430.00
Amount of bonds forfeited	600.00
Grand Total	$ 788,352.70

VIRGINIA ALCOHOLIC BEVERAGE CONTROL BOARD
DIVISION OF ENFORCEMENT
INVESTIGATOR'S SUNDAY OR HOLIDAY REPORT

DATE **4/16/66** DAY OF WEEK **Saturday**

NAME **R. F. Watkins** BASE **Tappahannock**

TERRITORY WORKED **Essex Co.**

NUMBER OF INVESTIGATIONS **1** NUMBER OF HOURS WORKED **15**

NUMBER OF RAIDS **2** NUMBER OF ARRESTS **3**

NUMBER OF STILLS **1** VALUE **$200.00**

NUMBER OF AUTOMOBILES SEIZED **1** VALUE **$100.00**

NUMBER OF TRUCKS SEIZED _____ VALUE _____

AMOUNT OF WHISKEY SEIZED _____ AMOUNT OF MASH SEIZED **300 Gal.**

COURTS ATTENDED _____ NUMBER OF CASES _____

HEARINGS ATTENDED _____ (Commissioner's, Grand Jury, Board, etc.) NUMBER OF CASES _____

PERSONS CONTACTED _____

OFFICERS AND TITLES ACCOMPANYING **ATU Bivins and Windsor**

ABC INVESTIGATORS OR INSPECTORS ACCOMPANYING **Birkett**

WHY WAS WORK NECESSARY TODAY? EXPLAIN WORK ATTEMPTED **Went back into the still located in the upper end of Essex county near Rustle and found it just as we left it. Continued to wait at the still. The violators came in and started to work. Raided the still and arrested three negro subjects at the time. Destroyed 1-50 gal. boiler, 2-50 gal wooden stills, 1-50 gal wooden doubler, 2-150 gal. mash boxes, 4-50 gal. mash barrels, 1-case of jars, copper lay worm and other misc. equipment. Seized one 1956 ford.**

COUNTY OR CITY	NO. OF RAIDS	NO. OF ARRESTS	NO. OF STILLS	NO. OF BUYS	NO. OF VEHICLES
Essex Co.	2	3	1		1

LEFT BASE **5a** RETURNED BASE **5p** LEFT BASE _____ RETURNED BASE _____

INVESTIGATOR

811-2 REV. 11/53

VIRGINIA ALCOHOLIC BEVERAGE CONTROL BOARD

DIVISION OF ENFORCEMENT

MONTHLY REPORT OF ACTIVITIES FOR September, 1967

I. Results of cases disposed of in September

Number of convictions	258
Number of dismissals	28
Number of cases not prosecuted	24
Number of interdictions	30
Amount of fines imposed	$ 11,390.00
Amount of fines suspended	$ 25.00
Total months jail sentences imposed	581
Total months jail sentences to serve	362
Total months jail sentences suspended	219
Number of defendants put under Bond	7
Amount of Bonds imposed	$ 2,500.00
Amount of Bonds forfeited	0

II. Stills, equipment etc., seized during September

Item	Price	Total Value
45 stills	Various prices	$ 15,782.00
6 automobiles	Various prices	2,195.00
2 trucks	Various prices	175.00
1,400 pounds sugar	$10.50 per hundred	147.00
860 pounds meal	$ 7.00 per hundred	60.20
100 pounds coke	$ 1.50 per hundred	1.50
141 cases of jars	$ 2.00 per case	282.00
39 55-gal. bbls.	$ 7.50 each	292.50
109 1-gal. jugs	$ .30 each	32.70
9 1-gal. cans	$ 1.00 each	9.00
Miscellaneous articles and equipment		1,265.85
544 gallons whiskey and 13,055 gallons mash reduced to whiskey at a ratio of 10:1, valued at $12.00 per gallon		$ 22,194.00
Total		$ 42,436.75
Amount of fines imposed		11,390.00
Amount of Bonds forfeited		0
Total		$ 53,826.75

III. Activities of Investigators

Number of investigations	2,417
Number of raids conducted	344
Number of arrests	239
Number of purchases for evidence	103
Number of days worked	1,506
Number of hours worked	10,358
Number of miles traveled	100,797
Number of counties worked in	90
Number of cities worked in	27

VIRGINIA ALCOHOLIC BEVERAGE CONTROL BOARD

DIVISION OF ENFORCEMENT

REPORT OF ACTIVITIES FOR FISCAL YEAR 1970-1971

Number of investigations conducted	26,894
Number of raids conducted - A.B.C. Violations	2,775
Number of raids conducted - Drug Violations	74
Number of raids conducted - Other Violations	112
Number of arrests - A.B.C. Violations	3,376
Number of arrests - Drug Violations	99
Number of arrests - Other Violations	1,105
Number of purchases from known violators - A.B.C. Violations	926
Number of purchases from known violators - Drug Violations	44
Number of purchases from known violators - Other Violations	1
Number of convictions	1,501
Number of dismissals	145
Number of cases nolle prosequi	75
Number of interdictions	62
Total fines imposed in State and Federal Courts	$ 93,585.75
Total fines suspended	$ 6,310.00
Total months jail sentences imposed	3,129
Total months jail sentences to serve	459
Total months jail sentences suspended	2,670
Number of defendants put under Peace Bonds	25
Amount of Bonds imposed	$ 17,400.00
Amount of Bonds forfeited	0
Number of gallons of whiskey seized	5,266
Number of gallons of mash seized and destroyed	114,635
Number of stills seized and destroyed	281
Number of vehicles seized	170
Number of pounds of sugar seized	10,710
Number of days worked	13,275
Number of hours worked	130,874
Number of miles traveled	1,182,751

The approximate value of the seizures listed above is as follows:

16,729.5 gallons whiskey at $12.00 per gallon (Mash seized and destroyed at stills condensed to whiskey at a ratio of 10:1)	$200,754.00
281 stills at various prices	$117,349.00
170 vehicles at various prices	$264,900.00
91,685 cans Beer at $.30 per can	$ 27,505.50
608 gallons Wine at $4.00 per gallon	$ 2,432.00
10,710 pounds sugar at $10.50 per hundred	$ 1,124.55
Miscellaneous articles and supplies	$ 14,340.65
Total	$628,405.70
Amount of fines imposed	$ 93,585.75
Amount of Bonds forfeited	0
Grand Total	$721,991.45

VIRGINIA ALCOHOLIC BEVERAGE CONTROL BOARD
DIVISION OF ENFORCEMENT
INVESTIGATOR'S DAILY REPORT

DATE __12/19/72__ DAY OF WEEK __Tuesday__
NAME __R. F. Watkins__ BASE __Tappahannock__
TERRITORY WORKED __Lancaster County.__
NUMBER OF INVESTIGATIONS __1__ NUMBER OF HOURS WORKED __6__
NUMBER OF RAIDS __2__ NUMBER OF ARRESTS __1__
NUMBER OF STILLS __2__ VALUE __$500.00__
NUMBER OF AUTOMOBILES SEIZED __1__ VALUE __$200.00__
NUMBER OF TRUCKS SEIZED _____ VALUE _____
AMOUNT OF WHISKEY SEIZED __16 gal.__ AMOUNT OF MASH SEIZED __400 gal.__
COURTS ATTENDED _____ NUMBER OF CASES _____
HEARINGS ATTENDED _____ (COMMISSIONER'S, GRAND JURY, BOARD, ETC.) NUMBER OF CASES _____
PERSONS CONTACTED _____
OFFICERS AND TITLES ACCOMPANYING _____
ABC INVESTIGATORS OR INSPECTORS ACCOMPANYING __Amos__

REMARKS __Went in to check the still located in Lancaster county near White Stone and found the still in operation at the time. Raided the still and arrested one negro subject. Destroyed two 30- gal copper stills, 2-3/4 inch copper coils, 1-½ inch copper coil, 2-55 gal. cooling barrels, 12-55 gal mash barrels, two gas burners, 2- five gal. plastic buckets, one bag of rye, 20- one gal. jars, 3- ½ gal jars, one shovel, one hoe, one hand drill, 1-30 gal drum, two hand pumps and seized one 1964 Dodge vehicle of which you will find a seizure form.__

COUNTY OR CITY	NO. OF RAIDS	NO. OF ARRESTS	NO. OF STILLS	NO. OF BUYS	NO. OF VEHICLES
Lancaster	2	1	2		1

LEFT BASE __3p__ RETURNED BASE __9p__ LEFT BASE _____ RETURNED BASE _____

INVESTIGATOR

811-1 REV. 11/53

Please present this to the probationers in State stores whats wrong that they law is at a stand still for these whiskey stills.

Search the woods through Occupacia Pedro, Passing district the woods leading on left going to Pedro & leading through the woods from Mt Olivet church of Husell you will find them through out the Essex & Caroline district.

its Transported all around fed up cant take it any longer Search Passing all the way up also homes dont wait

Dear ████████
I have some then to tell you that
happend on the Friday an Saturday
tell her to stop the first time
don't tell her that any one wrote
to you just find out for your
self ████████ tell with ███
and Bea on the Friday an Sat.
and Sunday Please stop her
Please! ~~Come by~~ go by
her house Friday night or Sat
People can't go to bed to late
at night I mean late at night
Stop her Pleas if she don't
Stop I will write you again
Please don't tell her that some
one wrote to you Pluse

Please
stop ~~[redacted]~~

Please don't take her
she sell Wishkey $3.00 a Pint
she Sell Beer 35¢ a Can
Chicken 50¢ 20¢ Hot

Please stop ~~[redacted]~~

I know because I seen
her sell it
its so say see for your self
don't tell I w rote this letter
Please Please dont tell who
wrote this letter

Selling

$3.00 Wiskey
and Beer
35¢

▬▬▬▬▬▬ is
selling Alcola. To People
that had to much to
drink- Also drinking on
Property side Toward
SCATING RING- MY HomE
BE Broke up on Rind This
He Never CLoSES Be FirE
1230- 1:30 AT NIGHT. SELL'S
IT AT ALL TIMES FRIDAY
NIGHT- WEED END You
CANT Find PlACE TO PARK.
PlEASE check iN To This
He ShouLD NoT BE AB
LE To SELL- Alchol oF
No, Kind PLACE NoT
FITTEW

PlEASE HELP ME.

I am reporting a still that is up in Hustle area. It may be on that Farm on 17 up above Vontens Church where all those big Grainy Bins at. It is a pond back in there all the way down on lower end of Farm. If it is not there it is in Hustle on ▇▇▇ place just above Harper Stone on right. I wish you all will put a End to this mess. because my boys just ~~to~~ drink all time from that Whiskey

Received 6-9-72
Time 8:45 A.M. By mail

april 22, 1968

Bobby:
Why don't you go to ▇▇▇ ▇▇▇ place and check on him. He is selling both kinds of whiskey their with his A.B.C. He is also selling beer on sunday's. He is keeping it in the back room of his store in some boxes I know he keeps the A.B.C. whiskey in their I dont know if he keeps the bootleg whiskey in their or not but people says are buying from him I think he sould be stopped. The best time to go their would be on the week end. ▇▇▇▇▇▇ are also selling bootleg whiskey too.

Thank you.

Dear Sir:

█████████ Store in Kinsale has been selling beer to minors. On Saturday and Sunday evenings teenagers from Callao come to █████ store because they get beer with no identification check. Last Sunday they must have sold beer to aleast seven or eight children under nineteen years old. I hate to see this go on because sooner or later on of these teenagers will probably get in an accident or hit someone while under the influence of alchol.

There is one other little problem. Beer is drank on the porch of the store during the weekend mostly. Plus it is also drank in the driveway.

The other stores in the nieghborhood don't sell to minors or let this type of foolishness go on. I don't see why █████ should be allowed to.

I'm old and set in my ways. I deserve a little piece of mind knowing that you will atleast look into this matter.

Westmoreland County 6/2/86

May be I should write the papers and people interested in this matter. Teenagers drinking isn't anything to laugh at. I know - I have already lost one grandson to it.

To Whom This May Concern:

Why is it that while driving up the Secondary Road by ▇▇▇ corner store in Kinsale my children and I should see men exposing their privates by taking leaks behind and around the store after they have had their fill of Beer?

Why is it that their beer bottles end up in the road where tires are just going to happen to be?

Why is it that the men are aloud to sit and drink in their cars where they just happen to block the road?

Why is it that ▇▇▇ allows them to throw their trash - bottles etc. in the field across from the store? This littering looks awful to the eyes.

Why is it these drunken men knock the signs by the

Life - like a home - needs love for its foundation.....
— J Carle Sexton

store down which just happen to be put up by the state department not more then a week or so?

When can the Virginia tax payers of this community expect something done about these promblems? It seems like the longer this problems go on the more embarrassing it becames because more and more goes on. ▇▇▇▇ should be able to handle the store or not sell beer which causes most of the promblems.

This is one Virginia tax payer asking you to please for myself and my children to look in to these problems.

Sept. 23, 1985

To Whom This May Concern:

I thought a lincense to sell beer off premises meant no beer drank on the property of store. ▮▮▮ Corner General in Kinsale seems to think otherwise around back of the store not even 6 ft. from a secondary road a group of men gather each day all day and drink. One day a man lay drunk on top of a car hood sleeping it off. Well, it's a disgrace I'm sick and tire off it. ▮▮▮ doesn't do anything about it because they buy plenty of beer from them.

What's wrong with you people. I thought you kept a check on such things. This has been going on for a while. May be you need to hire new people and fire the old.. You sure aren't doing your job.

~~A Concerned~~
A concerned
Citizen

Mr. Williams

Please excuse paper, but this is all I have at present.

I think you aught to know, there are people around the comunity peddlin dope, and selling whiskey that that they are transporting from Washington here.

Whiskey that was stolen from A,B,C stores during Dr. King's death

I got teen age boys an I hired a car, followed one by them Sunday to ▇▇▇ he went to Car. licsen #722692 an got a quart. While setting there I also saw others go to Car. license #722573 an do the same thing. I learned they go to ▇▇▇ at Clarsville on Saturday nite an Goldfield on Sunday's. I hope you send the law this week end with serch warrants, an catch these people if the people that own these places find it out, I am afraid they will tell it to some one, an you wont be able to catch them. I sugjest if you want to

Catch them at ▓▓▓▓ place, go Saturday night around 9:30 or 10 or ▓▓▓▓ about 2:30 Sunday an serch those car's, bath cor's are color green. An they were parked Sunday on the side of gold fild so the owner's could not see them. Please don't menion my name. ▓▓▓▓▓▓▓▓
P.S. I got one boy will try anything els he get any rope, I just well give up, if you are going to let it be like I tell you because bath car's are driven by women an they try's to be fast.

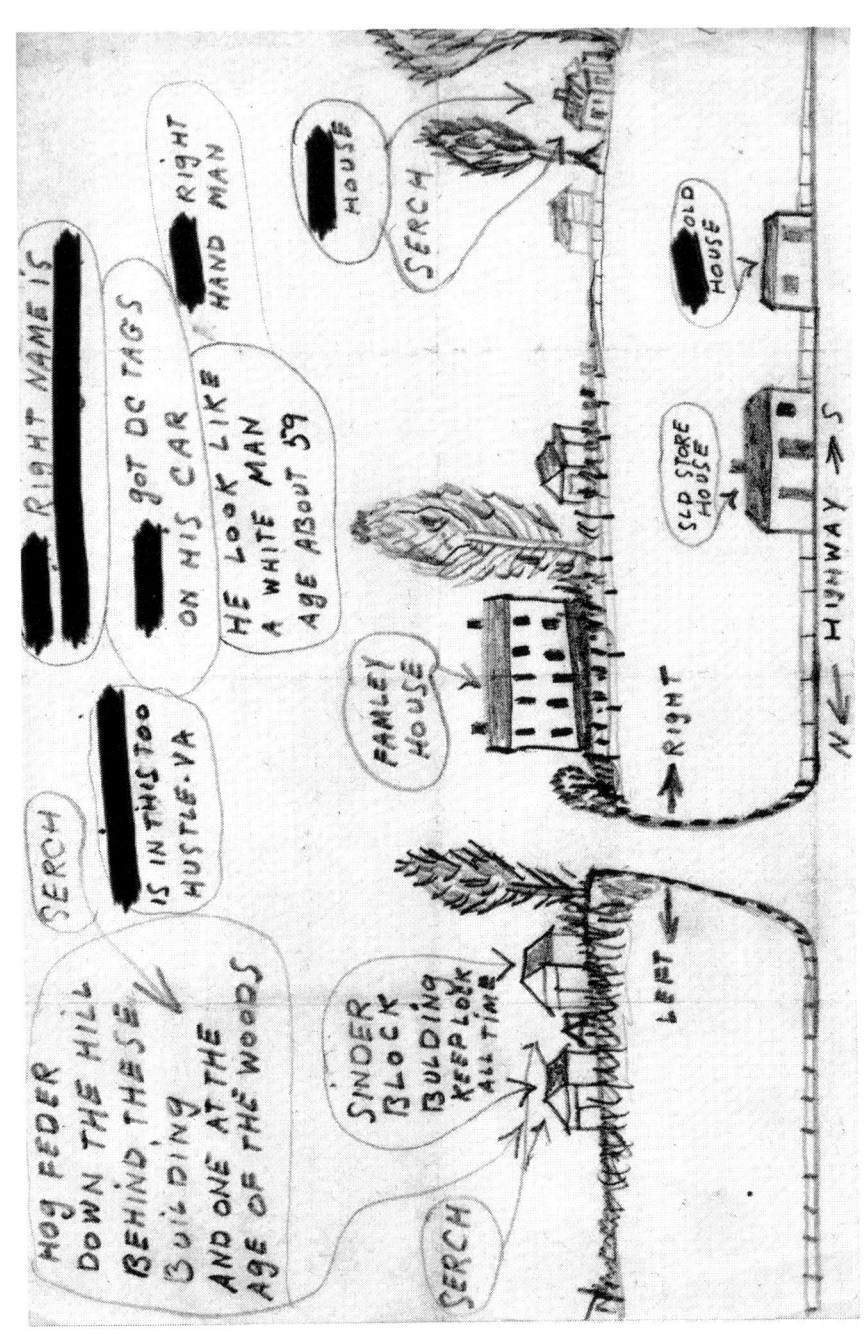

References

Economic History Encyclopedia, "Alcohol Prohibition," http://eh.net/encyclopedia.

Inside Spirits, a publication for employees of the Virginia Department of Alcoholic Beverage Control, March/April 2009, Volume 12, Number 2.

Moonshine: The Poison Business, Licensed Beverage Industries Inc., National Council Against Illegal Liquor, 1971.

The New Georgia Encyclopedia, "Temperance Movement," http://www.georgiaencyclopedia.org/nge/Article.jsp?id=h-828.

"Report on the Enforcement of the Prohibition Laws," National Commission of Law Observance and Enforcement, 1931.

Thank you for reading my stories.
I hope you have enjoyed the journey.

Made in the USA
Middletown, DE
09 April 2019